ADVANCE PRAISE FOR *MIR*

"*I never imagined/ I would ever* [...] Jane McKinney. I bet she and her daughter Mary McKSchmidt also never imagined they'd write about empty toilet paper shelves, advocating in hospitals, Mother Goose's eggs, slogans for going slow, and walkers. But as the title *Miracle Within Small Things* suggests, there is beauty, meaning, and connection to be found everywhere. What a beautiful offering, this book. I love how this mother/daughter pair weaves their love for each other through each page as together they explore loss, pain, fear, change, commitment, aging, loneliness, and love. Each poem and essayette is a testament to family, to creativity, and to the joy that comes in collaboration. *Miracle Within Small Things* is a gift.
Rosemerry Wahtola Trommer, author of *All the Honey* and *Hush*

There is remarkable tenderness in *Miracle Within Small Things*. A mother grapples with loss by focusing her writing on the smaller gestures of the natural world. A daughter, tending her, creates a rich multi-genre conversation with her mother's poems. Together, they interlace surviving without their beloveds into a web of meaning that affirms what it means to be beloved to each other. It is a beautiful book about a powerful bond.
Anne-Marie Oomen, author of *As Long as I Know You: The Mom Book* and other Michigan Notable Books awards

What a loving world it would be if all parents and their offspring sat down several times a week to chat. What would it be like to form a healing relationship, one meant to heal the rift imposed by a society that is simply too besieged by distractions, some unavoidable, from what personally matters. Then one day, well, it's too late. How many of us carry in our bag of regrets all the things "I never got around to asking"? Mary McKSchmidt didn't let that happen. *Miracle Within Small Things*, bravely composed by mother Jane McKinney and daughter Mary McKSchmidt, invites us into a conversation that, without lapsing into privacy or schmaltz, graciously offers a mother and daughter reflecting on what matters to all of us. Here's a collection of prose and poetry doing what it has always been meant to do—make accessible the great mysteries of hearts that have weathered our ineffable perceptions, insights, joys and sorrows. After being with this loving pair, you will wish you had or hope you will have what they call their times together, a "chair chat."

Jack Ridl, author of *Practicing to Walk Like a Heron*; co-recipient from *Foreword Reviews* of the award for the nation's best book of poetry

In *Miracle Within Small Things*, Jane McKinney and Mary McKSchmidt take each other's hand and describe (in poetry and prose) the stunning beauty of the natural world and their unique relationship. A quiet poignancy is reflected in their words that embrace life despite loss and grief. They teach us that ". . . every morning together is different, every morning together sacred" and we are blessed by the valuable insight of this mother, her daughter, and their tender bond.

Linda Nemec Foster, author of *Bone Country* and *The Blue Divide*

In *Miracle Within Small Things*, poets Jane McKinney and Mary McKSchmidt teach us how to deal with questions about fear and death and life transitions. This remarkable collection suggests that our answers can be found in the simplicity of nature and in the bonds of love that hold us together in the most challenging of times. More than anything, mother and daughter remind us of the importance of living with joy.

Eric Stemle, author of *I Was Not the Blossom: Growing with Your Students in a Nurturing Classroom*

Miracle Within Small Things, co-authored by mother/daughter team Jane McKinney and Mary McKSchmidt, awakens readers to magical moments in relationships, nature and life itself we too often miss in our busy lives. Both accomplished poets, writers, and lovers of nature, they describe how they've learned to live everyday with grace, gratitude, grit and humor as they grow older together, and invite us to share these miracle-filled moments with them.

Pamela H. Daugavietis, retired freelance writer, Grand Rapids, MI

Miracle Within Small Things

A Mother and Daughter's Journey

Through Loss and Aging

By Jane McKinney
and Mary McKSchmidt

MISSION POINT PRESS

Readers are encouraged to go to www.MissionPointPress.com to contact
the author or to find information on how to buy this book in bulk at a
discounted rate.

MISSION POINT PRESS

Published by Mission Point Press
2554 Chandler Rd.
Traverse City, MI 49696
(231) 421-9513
www.MissionPointPress.com

Design by Sarah Meiers

ISBN 978-1-958363-59-1 (Softcover)
ISBN 978-1-958363-58-4 (Hardcover)
ISBN 978-1-958363-67-6 (Large print, hardcover)

Library of Congress Control Number 2022923771

Printed in the United States of America

For my daughter
For my mother

Contents

Introduction xiii

Arizona

Sky Islands 3
Our Love Story 4
First Dinner Party 5
The Accounting Professor 7
Best Friends 9
Morning Walk 14
Just One Small Thing 15
A Monsoon Storm 16
I See His Reflection in the Water 18
Bird Watcher 20
Waiting.. 21
The Advocate 22
The Last Trip 25
Father's Day 27
Walking With Mary 30
A Loving Gesture 32
Our Pact.. 33
Lady's Spot 34
What Do Angels Look Like? 35
Healing.. 38
Falling Stars 39
Finding the Way... 40
Fear 41
Ash Monday 43
Watching Another Suffer... 44
Boxes... 45
The Day the Desert Rejoices 46
The Concert.. 47
Door Without a Lock... 48
Deep in My Heart.. 49
Losses 50

Michigan

The World I Left Behind 55

Desert to Wetlands 56

Outside My Window... 57

Autumn Leaves.. 58

Trappings 60

The Bribe... 61

Dealing with Loneliness 62

Beauty in Imperfection.. 64

Mother's Day 65

Nature's Encore 66

A Soothing Peace... 67

Playful Duck.. 68

Pioneer 69

The Wanderer.. 70

Lady-Two 71

The Swallowtail Speaks to the Poet... 72

They Come to Me 73

A Bird Visit... 74

Call of the Red-Winged Blackbird.. 75

Spring Snow 76

Voice of Mother Goose 77

Lost Sun.. 79

The Guardian 80

After She Tells Me She Loves Her Honda 81

Row of Red 82

My Birthday.. 83

Sunset.. 85

To Somebody's Father 86

New Slogan.. 88

She Knew Just What to Say 89

Problems 91

Magical Moment.. 92

The Sun.. 93

The Pandemic

The Poet Speaks to the Swallowtail... 97

Winter Reigns 98

Prayer for the Caregivers 99

Her Heart Was in the Sugar 100

A Gray Day 101

Our Time 102

Why Toilet Paper? 103

A Blank Mind 104

The Wind 105

Tilley Hat 107

Peace and Tranquility 109

Surviving 110

Unhappy Squirrel 111

The Breakfast Bench 113

The World Around Us 115

Escaping Geese 116

Learning Another Language 118

An Unusual Gift 120

Fourteen Days 121

He is Not Here 123

A Daughter's Thoughts on Compression Stockings 125

Promise of Spring 126

No Leisurely Stroll 127

Where Are the Ducks? 129

Conflict 130

Chair Chat

It's Spring 133

Were It Not for the Moon 135

Under a Bushel Basket 136

Turquoise Plaid Pajamas 138

The Blossom 139

Miracle Within Small Things 140

The Jane Tree 141

The 'Girl' on Windmill Island 142

Legacies 144

Special Plants 145

On Bad Days 146

A Lost Boy 147

Resolution 149

Joy in My Heart..150

Three-Letter Word 151

Family 153

Have I Told You Enough? 155

Sign of Winter 156

Remembering 157

Yesterday and Today 159

After Receiving the Distressing Letter 160

The Royal View..161

Disappointed 163

Pride 165

Early Morning 166

Poets at Play 167

Total Well-Being..168

When?..169

A Prized Gift...171

Invisible 172

After the Flight from Albuquerque 173

Buds and Birds 174

Why Am I Here? 176

That Morning in the Hospital 178

My Next-to-Best Friend......................................179

Turning Point 180

Dear Mother..181

A Lost Fight...182

A Respite..183

Lady 184

Preparing..186

A Perfect Picture..187

Determine 189

My Best Friend...191

Epilogue 192

In Gratitude 195

Introduction

Daughter: Usually, I pull the butter from the fridge so it can soften for her toasted muffin, place the newspaper on the table, put my purse on the couch, open the blinds in the living room, and listen for the creek of the recliner in which she sleeps, the rattling of blinds in her bedroom, and watch for the corresponding splash of daylight sweeping across her walls.

Then I walk down the hall to her room.

Mother: I open the blinds when I hear her, look out the window to see if the sun is peeking around the corner of the building, glance at the Wanderer, the Berry-Bird tree, the hydrangea bush, and then wait for my daughter to walk in the room. She stoops to where I sit in my recliner and kisses me before sliding down the bed to the floor. Always, she is smiling.

First, she asks me how my night went. If there is something exciting, like a fire alarm at 6:30 in the morning, I tell her. No one gets scared any more at these alarms. Too many false ones. She asks me what I did—step by step. I tell her. Touched the door to see if it was hot. Put my shoes on. Put on my coat. Grabbed my keys and cane. Checked the door again. Stepped into the hall, turned left, and walked out the building. She's up and kisses me again, pleased that I did everything perfectly. And then she slides back down the bed to the floor.

Daughter: Because I'm nearing seventy, the easiest way to get to the floor is to slide down the side of the bed. Once there, our chair chat begins. Now an essential part of our lives, these intimate conversations first officially began the night of the moon, the night I walked into her room and discovered her sleeping, face pointed to the sky. Prior to that, our mother/daughter conversations were more random, usually taking place on our outdoor adventures when my to-do lists for her were left on the kitchen counter.

Sometimes we talk about what's happening outside the bedroom window or what's scheduled for the day. The best mornings are when we both have been productive the day before, when each of us can share a draft of something we wrote. That's usually a catalyst for a thoughtful conversation that extends far beyond our normal thirty minutes. Like the dawn breathing light into eastern skies, every morning together is different, every morning together sacred.

Arizona

Sky Islands

For over twenty years I visited my parents in Tucson without knowing scientists consider it part of the Sky Island Region, 70,000 square miles where mountains tower over 6,500 feet and jut above the desert floor like "islands on the ocean." I saw a desert valley of windswept browns and muted greens, a skyline defined by ragged, seemingly impregnable mountains. I did not consider it a place I might find nourishment, an environment in which I might heal.

I was wrong.

For two years following the death of my dad and their dog, Lady, Mother remained in Arizona. I spent many months with her, often accompanied by my husband, Rubin. While she rested and Rubin played pool, I hiked the trails of the Rincon, Santa Catalina and Santa Rita Mountains. I explored the Tucson Mountains west of the city, not tall enough to technically be labeled one of the Sky Islands but a familiar backdrop to the blushing skies of sunset. While I preferred to photograph the exuberance of spring, I could not ignore the charred skeleton of the saguaro, the feathered remains of the coyotes' feast, the lifeless rodent dangling from the beak of a roadrunner.

Life is not always the strawberry pink of the hedgehog petals.

Like the seeds of the brittlebush scattered across the parched sand, the lessons of the desert sprouted roots within the dry crevices of my heart. Life struggling, persevering, blossoming, dying. I was part of that desert story. With each click of the camera, I began to heal.

Our Love Story

Across the classroom, four rows back
I feel his eyes upon me.
My young heart quivers, then races.
It never recovers.

A junior high party . . . spin the bottle . . .
an embarrassed, almost silent
walk around the block.
Do we hold hands?
Do we edge close together?
What do we say?

A high school hallway
jammed with noisy students . . .
he comes up beside me.
I hear only the question, "Go steady?"
I nod my head.

Tall and handsome in his Navy blues,
he holds my hand and pleads,
"Please wait for me."
I promise I will.

Side by side
beneath an archway of flowers . . .
he in tux and me in shimmering white . . .
we promise to love one another
until death do us part.

We did. And it did.

First Dinner Party

A new bride . . .
Our first dinner guests . . .
I try not to panic.

My version of Mom's
famous silver plate pot roast
looks as appetizing as hers.
The table is elegant with
wedding gift china and silver.
One last look . . . a deep breath.

I invite my husband and guests
to the dining room.
Their first sight of the table
elicits a chorus of oohs and aahs.
I puff up with pride and relief.

Suddenly, a low, grinding noise . . .
We watch in stunned horror
as the right leaf of the table
slowly gives way.
Food and dishes crash to the floor.

I cannot speak. I cannot think.
My husband puts his arm around me,
gives our guests money and asks them
to bring burgers back for dinner.

While he mops up the mess,
I let the tears flow. Then he holds me close
and makes everything all right.

...

The burgers on paper plates
taste delicious.

The Accounting Professor

For T. Harry McKinney, 8/20/1925-10/7/2012

He could have been a coach,
he recalls, idly fingering
the Rose Bowl ring
just pulled from the tattered
chocolate candy box he keeps
in the middle drawer of his dresser.
He remembers that first
touchdown pass in high school,
the eruption of the crowd, the smiles
in the hallway the next morning.
No one ever again called him
"white trash," accused him
of being from the wrong side
of Fourth Street.

It had been a tough decision.
Coaching or teaching. But
if he became a teacher, he could help
even the short, skinny kids
cross Fourth.

He pulls the game ball, given to him
by his buddies, from behind the books
in the closet. He grips it tightly,
remembering the dean's reprimand
earlier in the day: "Too many students
doing too well in your Accounting 101 class."

...

He's told to adjust his curve, fail more students,
shrink the number daring to dream
they can graduate from this prestigious
school of business. His job, he's reminded,
is to weed out the unworthy.

He returns the ring to its rightful place,
but the game ball, signed by every coach and player
of that national championship team,
he carries to the kitchen table and
places beside the stack of papers waiting
to be graded. "I could have been a coach,"
he mutters aloud, "but I know
I'm a damn good professor."

Best Friends

My husband, Harry, sat listlessly turning pages in a fishing magazine that had just arrived in the mail.

Suddenly: "I want a dog."

I stared at him. "You what?"

Again: "I want a dog."

"We're retired," I reminded him. "We certainly don't need the responsibility of a dog."

He turned the magazine around to face me. A full-page picture showed a man standing in a stream fly-fishing. Close beside him stood a sleek, shining golden retriever.

What could I say? Fishing trips for my husband date back to memorable childhood outings with his dad and, later, to summer trips with close buddies. But clinical depression, an inherited illness which worsened with retirement, kept him home looking at magazines instead of wading in streams. He told me he could not push through the invisible wall that hemmed him in, a wall that isolated him from people and activities.

A picture in a fishing magazine appeared to be prying open a small crack in that wall.

For several months, Harry visited humane shelters and pet stores searching for his dog. While he seemed to enjoy looking, he never found the right one. I wondered if he ever would. After all, he had a mixed history with dogs. As a young naval officer, Harry had endured a series of rabies shots after the ship's mascot, a dog, developed rabies. He shivered when describing the horror of having a long needle jabbed into his stomach every morning for two weeks.

"Absolutely no dogs for our children," he declared many years later. "Too risky."

Then, one day he invited our three younger children to go with him on an errand.

"Guess what, Mom," the children yelled as they banged through the front door on their return, "Look what we have!" The oldest of the three cradled a puppy in her arms. My husband grinned.

"It's the $10 dog from the pound. We thought about bringing his brother too, but we settled for one."

The children named the dog Rusty. A golden retriever-mix, he ruled our family for fifteen years. But even when Rusty raced and chased with the children, he never failed to sense my husband's low times. The dog would stop playing, go to my husband sitting forlornly in his recliner and nuzzle against his knee.

Perhaps the memory of Rusty's apparent empathy spurred my husband's current interest in owning a dog again. At any rate, one Saturday morning Harry called from the pet store.

"I've found my dog. A golden retriever-mix. Come see her."

She lay on her side stretched out on the floor. In no way did she resemble the sleek, shining dog in the fishing magazine picture.

"She's depressed," explained Alicia, the humane shelter employee who brought her to the pet store for possible adoption. "Not only did her previous owner abuse her, but he also took her three-week-old puppies from her to sell, then dropped her at the shelter."

I sat on the floor beside the dog, petting her head and whispering loving words. No response. She stared straight ahead with big, sad eyes. Her bones poked out against the skin on her back. Her hair hung dull and dingy.

"This is her third visit for possible adoption," Alicia said. "If it doesn't happen today, shelter rules call for the dog to be put to sleep."

Harry bent down to pat the dog gently. He looked over at me. "Let's take her home with us and see what we can do for her."

Harry named his dog Lady. When he introduced us to her as Gran and Granpa, she looked at the floor instead of us. Most of the time Lady huddled in her crate staring sadly into space. When Harry placed a bowl of food in front of her, she turned her head away. He took some dry dog food in his hand, urging her to take a taste.

"You have to eat to grow strong, Lady, so you can be my fishing buddy," he pleaded. "It'll soon be fishing season."

Little by little, Harry managed to get her to eat. But she still would not look at him, even when he petted her or called her "my sweet, little sweetie."

My heart ached for both Lady and my husband as I watched the dog unable to respond to his love.

Harry had to coax Lady to walk with him. She crept along so slowly that sometimes he had to pull hard on the leash to get her to move. When anyone approached them, Lady ducked behind Harry, refusing to acknowledge even the kindest words.

It took three weeks before Harry and Lady returned from a walk with Harry smiling triumphantly.

"I think we've turned a corner," he reported with relief. He told me the story.

They had walked up the hill near our house, and a rabbit had scurried out of the wash and stopped close to them. Immediately, Lady stiffened and began to shake. Guessing she had been abused for chasing rabbits, Harry knelt down beside her, drawing her quivering body close to him.

"Bunny rabbits are your friends," he soothed. "You don't hurt them, and they don't hurt you." He patted her gently as they watched the rabbit together. When the rabbit scampered away, Lady turned her head toward Harry and, finally, looked straight into his eyes.

That walk was a turning point. After that, every time Lady heard the garage door open, her ears perked up and her tail thumped on the floor as she waited for him to come into the house.

"How's my sweet, little sweetie?" Harry greeted her. When he bent to pet her, she nuzzled against his leg.

I often heard Harry sing-song to her as he rubbed her tummy. "Rubba-rubba-rubba, puppies in a tubba. Who do you think they be? Why it's Lady and Rusty waiting for me."

How different from the days he had sat for hours with eyes closed and shoulders drooping. Now, a smile lighted his face as he watched Lady running to him. Sometimes she brought a toy for tug-a-war. Often, she came to sit quietly beside him, his hand on her head while he read.

I felt both relief and joy as I watched the bond of love growing between them, a bond bringing comfort and pleasure to both.

"Lady never barks," Harry observed one day. Concerned, he stopped by the humane shelter.

"She was severely punished for barking in her previous home and may never bark again," Alicia warned. "But there's a chance if she gains enough confidence in you, her bark will return."

Lady soon warmed to me, but she remained fearful of strangers. When she and Harry walked and anyone tried to befriend her, she scooched close to Harry and buried her head in his leg.

One fellow walker, Stan, wouldn't give up trying to become Lady's friend. He always talked to her quietly, offering his hand but never forcing her to accept it.

"I once had a dog named Duke, Lady," Stan told her one day. "I used to talk to him about everything. When I had a problem to solve or when something really nice happened, I told Duke about it."

Lady turned her head toward Stan as though she understood every word. This time when he held out his hand, Lady leaned into it for a pat on her head. After that, Lady always greeted him with wagging tail, sitting to get her neck massaged and rolling over for a tummy rub.

With other people, Lady remained distant and fearful.

Her behavior with rabbits changed drastically. No fear anymore. When one dashed out of the desert wash or from under a nearby bush, Lady yanked at the leash as though she would chase it. Harry held hard, and she settled for standing on her back legs, dancing a victory dance when the rabbit scampered away.

One day I saw Lady follow Harry into the garage. She watched curiously as he opened a cabinet door, pulled out his favorite fly rod and swished it expertly through the air.

"It's almost fishing season, Lady. This is what I use to catch fish."

He grinned at her then took a small box from the cabinet and emptied it. He put her yellow tennis ball, her stuffed teddy bear and a handful of her treats into the box.

"This is your tackle box, Lady. You can't go fishing without a tackle box." He held it low so she could see inside. She sniffed it. She thumped her tail. She cocked her head to one side to look up at him.

And she gave one short bark.

Harry caught his breath and bent to hug her. "We're going fishing real soon, Lady, and we'll take your tackle box with us."

But Lady didn't get to go fishing with her Granpa and her tackle box.

Instead, one night she cowered in her crate and anxiously watched the yellow-clad firemen and paramedics work on her Granpa, eventually carrying him out the front door. Cradling Lady's head in my hands, I explained they were taking Granpa to the hospital.

Harry suffered a small stroke which left him, among other things, with a lack of balance. This meant Lady needed a new walking partner.

As Lady and I walked up the hill early one morning during the first week of our new partnership, I said, "Oh, Lady, just look at the beautiful sky." I pointed to the pink, gold and coral colors meshing together to usher in the Arizona day. While we stood admiring it, a mockingbird atop an ocotillo bush sang out its appreciation. Lady cocked her head to listen. Right then I knew we would be great walking partners.

Morning Walk

When the sun's
    warm touch rids
        early morning of its frost

When the gentle breeze
    pushes away the lingering
        coldness of the night

When the awakening birds
    fill the air with
        cheerful songs of greeting

When eager, smiling Lady
    joins me for our
        daily morning walk

My heart is full.

Just One Small Thing

Closing time
at the Gift Shop.
Sign taken down.
Door locked.
Cash register closed.
Lights off.
Time to leave.

A light rap on the door.
I unlock it.
A woman asks:
Will you sell me
just one small thing?
Closed, I want to tell her
but I smile and say sure.

For my daughter's birthday
the woman adds
reaching past me
for a little book off the shelf:
"Lady . . . A Love Story."

A Monsoon Storm

A storm rages in the night.
Lightning crackles.
Thunder booms.
Rain pelts the earth.

Lady does not like it.

Prowling room to room
her rapid panting echoing
through the dark
she barks a fearful plea for help.

Come Lady, I call from the bedroom.
She pokes her chin up on my pillow.
I cradle her head in my arms
assuring her: The storm will not hurt you, Lady.

Unbelieving, she creeps over
to my husband,
slips her nose under his arm,
repeats her fearful bark.
He assures her: The storm will not hurt you, Lady.

Still unbelieving, she returns to me.
Then to him. Then to me. Then to him.
I fall asleep.

When I awake, the storm is over.
I am alone.
In the living room,
my husband is asleep on the recliner,
his arm draped protectively over Lady.

The storm did not hurt Lady.

I See His Reflection in the Water

I suspect he was awake most of the night worrying about his fifty-five-year-old daughter camping alone in the White Mountains of Arizona.

"I lugged two tents through two airports and flew across the country to go fishing with you in Show Low," I said. "You don't have to go with me, but I'm leaving tomorrow at 7:00 a.m."

I didn't fully understand his depression, didn't recognize the early signs of dementia. I knew only that our spirited debates over coffee were fewer, and he was becoming more withdrawn in his recliner.

I wasn't ready to let him go.

Dad watched silently as I crammed a dome tent for him and pup tent for me into the jeep I'd rented; hauled his bulky patio recliner, the chair in which he frequently slept, from the back porch to the trunk; added a ground pad and sleeping bag for me, fishing poles, cooler, and duffel.

I see his reflection in the water: both of us with blonde hair, square chins, broad shoulders. But our similarities go beyond looks. I, like him, am strong-willed, fiercely independent, competitive, with a keen interest in learning, determined to make a difference in the world. I also inherited the big "R" for responsibility, particularly when it involves family, and his propensity to worry—especially about family, individuals over whom we have little to no control.

Like me. Like the time I skipped off to Africa against his wishes, $200 in my pocket and midway through my college education. Or my steadfast insistence on playing ice hockey—with guys. Or four months ago, when I packed my car with camping gear, backpack, computer and camera and hiked alone up the coast of Lake Michigan. I was in transition and needed time to think and he, the man who had introduced me to camping, who was also an explorer, an introvert, and a thinker, he understood. But he feared for my safety.

As I feared for his. I remember finding him that morning after his first night in a hospital room, blood soaking his gown, bedrail inadvertently left down, call button ignored by an overworked staff reeling from labor shortages. Never again did he spend a night alone in a hospital. Different procedures, different hospitals, but never alone.

At 7:00 a.m. the morning of our camping trip, I saw his tall, stooped frame dressed in his familiar, worn, gray plaid flannel shirt and baggy slacks shuffling toward the jeep. A small toiletries case was in one hand, his tackle box in the other. And while he watched me assemble the two tents in Arizona gale winds, watched me lug his chair to the tent so he could awaken to a view of the lake, he chose to sleep in the jeep. In hindsight, I should have asked. The car was safer for him. Paved path to the bathroom. A car horn available should something go wrong. Fewer worries.

I don't regret that I pressured him into taking that last camping trip. He, like me, was at peace in nature. And it had been a long time since I'd seen him at peace. My only regret is that I waited so long to ask for his help in tying flies. I tied the only knot I knew: a bowline. While ideal for securing a forty-foot sailboat to a dock, it was useless in securing a miniscule, lighter-than-an-ounce fly to a fishing line. When we returned, his tackle box was empty. Not even a bite to brag about. A tired smile on both our faces.

Bird Watcher

Stretched out on the patio wall
Lady watches the birds next door.

Pecking and scratching the ground
squabbling over spots at the feeders
racing from one feeder to another
the birds think only of their hunger.

A huge, glossy, black crow
swoops down from a tree
scattering birds in every direction
to seek safety in bushes and trees.

The crow, satisfied with frightening
the birds but not savoring bird food
gives a raucous call and flies away.

Instantly, the birds are back
squabbling over the feeders.

Soon a roadrunner, tail stretched high
races into their midst, sending them
back into the bushes and trees.

Deciding birds have a hard life
Lady slips down from the wall.

Waiting

First thing every morning
    Lady checks the chair
        my husband always sits in.

        It's empty.

Puzzled, she walks slowly
    from room to room
        then back to his chair.

She sits close beside it
    waiting to feel his hand
        stroking her head.

The Advocate

I.
No, you are not moving my dad
to another floor where the nurses are not
as experienced managing pain
and yes, I get that this floor
is for orthopedic patients
and that orthopedic surgeons are second
only to the cardiovascular guys
in generating revenue to this hospital,
but my dad is in excruciating pain
suffering simultaneously
from C. *Diff* and sepsis, both infections
he got while in this hospital,
most likely triggered by staff
who did not wash their hands correctly,
and because treating one
spikes the severity of the other
there is nothing you can do for him
but manage his pain, so, no,
you are not transporting him
anywhere but to hospice
where his wife, who had no idea
he would die from this hospital admission,
can sit in something other than this stick chair
from which she can now barely move,
begin the grieving process without
seeing her husband's face contorted in pain
and where they can have their dog, Lady,
at their side, and if you try to move him
anywhere else, I will throw my Irish body
on the floor in front of this door

and throw a fit unlike anything you've seen
and if you need me to explain all this
to the head nurse, the orthopedic chair
or the CEO of this hospital I will gladly do so
but until a bed opens up in hospice,
my dad is going
nowhere.

II.
The physician had accepted this position
as hospitalist to help families like this one
navigate the bureaucratic hallways
of the medical center. And while he had

obtained a bed on the orthopedic floor
for the night, she was right,
her father should be in hospice.
But even he could not manufacture a bed,

nor could he move her dad to the top of the list.
But he knew someone who could
and scheduled an interview that morning.
The rest was up to the daughter.

Three days later, the hospitalist sipped his coffee
staring at skies aglitter with stars and constellations
he could not name but relished in these few
moments before his day began.

He fingered the mug, the ceramic as familiar
as the son who gifted it to him those years ago,
when he embarked on a journey aligned
with his passion, not his pocketbook.

There were times he regretted the decision
to leave private practice, when egos and red tape

...

smothered his resolve to shoulder the weight
crushing those he was committed to serve.

But then he'd get an email, like the one
he just opened, about that old man
and his Irish daughter. He stood up.
It was time to go to work.

The Last Trip

He cannot speak but he can hear.
I scoot my chair close to his bed,
take his hand in both of mine
and talk of our life together.

His eyes never leave mine
as I describe our school days,
the separation of war years,
our marriage, our six children.

He enjoyed traveling,
particularly to the mountains
where his spirit always soared.
So I reminisce about his favorite trips
to Colorado and Switzerland.

Then I talk about the Hawaiian Islands
where we visited to celebrate his retirement.
I'm sure he smiles as I recount our
surprise and delight when we were
given the immense and elegant
"Honeymoon Suite" at the hotel in Hilo.

When an hour passes, our daughter
urges me to take time for breakfast.
I take only a few bites
when I notice a change in his breathing.
I move quickly to his bedside.
There is indeed, a drastic change.

. . .

Our daughter, our son and our dog
join me beside him
as he takes his last breath.

Father's Day

He rarely talked about playing football for Southern
California, about what it was like to start on offense *and* defense
on the 1944 Rose Bowl Championship team. What I do
remember is that he was in constant pain from injuries to his
spine and that he never encouraged his sons to play the game.

My dad died October 7, 2012, at the age of eighty-seven.
But I began losing him in 2006, the year he fell and broke his hip,
when the combination of anesthesia and an error in post-surgery
pain medication seemed to muddy his brilliant mind. That was
before scientists discovered the link between football injuries to
the head and chronic traumatic encephalopathy (CTE), a disease
that can lead to aggression, depression, anxiety, and eventually,
progressive dementia. That was before I discovered his football
photographs and realized helmets in the 1940s were dog-eared
contraptions made of leather, and so much about my dad became
clear. That was before I learned dementia squeezes oxygen from
the brain and can result in paranoia and preposterous accusations.
That was before I realized dementia can result in the three Rs:
increasing *repetition*, difficulty with *recall*, the near impossibility
of *reason*. That was before I learned that in some people, like Dad,
dementia creates a fourth R: *Rage*.

By late autumn of 2011, it was no longer safe for Dad to live
at home physically because of daily falls, or mentally because of
the heightened state of dementia. There was no choice but to place
him in an assisted living facility against his will.

Against his will.

His demons, unleashed and unchecked as the condition
progressed, lashed out at me. The ferocity of his fury felt like he
was pounding his fist in my face, choking the last bit of air from
my lungs, taking a knife to my heart. The memories shadowed me
like the blackest of monsoon skies above Arizona, following me

home to Michigan, creating my own swirl of demons to haunt the nights.

Mother will tell you she has had an easy life. I know differently. She chooses the memories to carry with her so as to live with joy. "Whatever you carry becomes a part of you," she warns.

Despite suffering from depression most of his adult life, my dad did his best to be there for me. It was he who introduced me to the thrill of a Lake Michigan sunset, to the adventures of camping; he who taught me the art of tying flies and mending lines, who stressed education as a way to open doors and emphasized a responsibility for advocating for those less fortunate. He told me to stand tall in the presence of others; that mediocrity was unacceptable and success required commitment and hard work. It was my dad who showed me I could make a difference, as he had in my life, the lives of his students, and the many young people to whom he made education available and affordable through his work with state and federal legislators.

I remember sitting next to his hospital bed that October, waiting for transport to Peppi's House, the hospice facility on the Tucson Medical Center Campus. I fought hard to get him that room, a place Mother could sleep on the pullout couch at his side; where his cherished dog, Lady, could wander from his bed to the little patio outside; where I could, for the last time, advocate on his behalf.

My hand in his as we waited for transport, my tears soaked his hospital gown as I recalled my favorite memories . . . the time we walked together, hand-in-hand, to the Red Cedar River to feed the ducks; playing rambunctious rounds of Clue as a family; his smile when he decoded our cryptic engagement announcement; walking me down the aisle and his toast at our wedding; our fishing trips to the Snake River and Show Low, Arizona; his ongoing hunt for spare golf balls in the scrub off the fairway; his willingness to treat me to Starbucks coffee, rather than McDonald's, as we thrashed out our different perspectives on life, death, politics . . . until I noticed his jaw trembling, his breathing labored. I paused and placed my head close to his.

In a choking voice he whispered his last words. "I love you, Mary."

This is the dad I carry in my heart.

Walking With Mary

Lady's walks become a wonder world
when Mary comes to visit.

The path up the hill with a desert wash on each
side of the road becomes *Coyote Trail*
with Mary urging Lady to be on the lookout
for coyotes crossing from one side to the other.

On *Lake Loop*, while admiring the pond
down the street, Mary describes to Lady
the fun and danger of the immense lake
Mary lives beside in Michigan.

Lady stops for a drink of water from her own
blue cup at *Bobcat Bench*, and Mary meets
the bobcat sitting on the wall across the street
with whom Lady always has a stare-down.

One of Lady's favorite walks is *Grass Hill*
where she tries Mary's patience by never
wanting to quit nibbling the bright, green grass
growing along the sidewalk.

Mary and Lady agree they feel anxious when
they walk on *Javelina Haunt* because they
once saw a javelina grazing in the front yard of
one of the houses there.

Sunrise Stretch is a walk Mary and Lady
avoid when the weather is hot because
it is an area where no shade is available.

And a walk they absolutely will not take anymore is *Poison Path* because Lady became sick to her stomach twice after eating something toxic there.

Lady always enjoys her walks but they are more fun than ever when Mary holds the leash.

A Loving Gesture

Lady sits quietly in a chair beside me
waiting to see the veterinarian.
Okay, Lady, you can come
with me now, the technician says.

Lady puts her paw on my arm and
leans her head on my shoulder.
I catch my breath in thrilled surprise.

Then Lady jumps down from the chair
and follows the technician.

Our Pact

Holding her close
I whisper to Lady:
whether few or many
days remain
each is a special
sharing of love
and caring.

She touches my arm
tenderly with her tongue
to seal our pact.

Lady's Spot

Outside my kitchen window
three oleander bushes clump
tightly together, their leaves
snuggling close to the ground—
except in one small spot
where Lady has smoothed out
a shallow resting place.

On this morning
Lady struggles to the spot
drops to the ground
stretches out on her side.
She smiles. Her eyes close.

Birds overhead sing Lady's requiem.

DAUGHTER

What Do Angels Look Like?

My prayers fly across the dry desert wash, soaring up the ragged tops of the Catalina Mountains until finally touching the pink whisper of dawn. I pray to the spirits of all the great women who have gone before me that they might provide me insight, compassion, forgiveness, and strength.

Above all, I beg for strength.

For seven weeks I have jogged to this isolated cul-de-sac, breaking stride to pause, admit my vulnerability, ask for help. This morning I cannot stop the warm, salty tears from silently spilling over my cheeks and dropping to the dry earth beneath my feet. I have not the energy to brush them away. Death has depleted my spirit, robbed me of all I need to see clearly, to find joy in the little things. Even the wildflowers.

It is not my dad's death I mourn, nor my father-in-law's. Both died peacefully, welcoming death after so many years suffering the pain of chronic illness. There is a void and a sadness that I should lose both in so short a span of time. But the emptiness I feel this morning is for another.

I miss the jangling tags of Lady.

Her soft, freshly brushed fur, the color of autumn, is imprinted on my palms. I see her eagerly greeting me, urging me to walk with her, to breathe the crisp desert air, to scour every inch of land within four feet of the sidewalk, to pause and watch a rabbit scurrying for cover, to eye a cardinal chirping from a nearby mesquite tree, to relish every moment of life.

I have never been a dog lover. When I was a child, my father warned me to avoid dogs. He recounted vividly the pain he experienced as a Navy ensign, the fourteen shots in the stomach received after diving overboard to rescue the ship's mascot, a dog that tested positive for rabies. I remember my terror walking home in second grade when a black Labrador tore after me.

Trembling, I hid behind a bush until his interest waned and he bounded off to pursue another. Forty-five years later, a pack of six dogs landed me in an ambulance after I was attacked while jogging the sidewalks of a small Michigan community, a town with a leash law the owner chose to ignore. A jagged scar cuts across my back.

The scar digs deeper than skin.

Lady, the dog rescued by my dad to be his fishing buddy, sensed my fear and kept her distance until I was called to my parents' side to help them through the heart-wrenching, physically cruel dimensions of aging. It was Lady who knew intuitively I was exhausted, that while I wanted to be strong for my grieving mother, my father's dementia-fueled anger was ripping through me, crushing my spirit. Late at night as I sat on the floor sleepless, churning with responsibility, emotionally drained, it was the sixty-four-pound golden retriever mix that gently nudged her body next to mine, tapping the floor with her tail to remind me I was not alone.

The tears blind my eyes as the sun's rays spray light above the mountains and the wispy pink clouds fade to a deep violet. I still see Lady's sparkling eyes peering up at Dad in the unfamiliar hospice room, hear her footsteps trotting down the hallway repeatedly to console my mother the weeks after his death. I feel her tugging the leash to teach me to jaywalk, to show me her favorite routes, the pace she most preferred. But most of all, I hear the clanking of tags every morning I sip coffee under starlit skies, waiting for dawn; every evening Mother and I watch the sun paint the craggy Catalina Mountains pink.

Six weeks after Dad died, lymphoma overwhelmed Lady's body. I remember rolling little balls of food and feeling her weary tongue on my fingers, cupping water in my hands and begging her to drink. When she became agitated with pain, I brushed her for hours as I recounted all my favorite memories. Near midnight her last night, Lady insisted on going outside—as if reminding me a lady never does her business indoors. She dragged her hind legs to her favorite place before collapsing in exhaustion. "You can't stay here," I begged. "Listen to the coyotes."

She could not move.

I dashed inside and grabbed a comforter, gently rolled her body onto the soft fabric and gingerly pulled her to the nearby porch. Her breathing was fast, difficult, too consuming for her to help me lift her into the house, a place she'd be safe, a place I thought she could die in comfort.

The biting wind of the desert echoed with the whooping of coyotes. Grabbing plastic lawn chairs, I built a barricade around Lady to protect her from the wild. Wrapped in a blanket to shield me from the frigid night air, a broom for a weapon, I began pacing. If the coyotes were to creep through the blackness of a moonless night, they'd have to confront this fiercely protective sentry first.

Two hours later, shrill cries howling from the desert wash across the street jolted me into reality and I clumsily lifted Lady inside. Mother joined the vigil and Lady immediately lifted her tired head to acknowledge the soft, cooing voice, a nurturing sound familiar to us both.

Mother and I took turns brushing the soft, auburn fur until the light of dawn replaced the night and Lady insisted on returning outdoors. She dragged her body across the stones to a small hole she'd dug years ago beneath an oleander bush. It was a place she felt safe, where she could watch the birds fluttering in the branches as they came to say goodbye, a place she could hear the whispers of Mother and me as we stroked her weary body.

Several hours later, brushed and beautiful beneath her favorite bush, Lady's labored breathing stopped. She died quietly and in peace. Just like my dad.

The tears trickle down my face as I feel the desert warming under the morning sun. Before resuming my jog, I say a prayer to the strongest spirit I have known, a four-legged creation of God who mirrored all the goodness, the joy, the inquisitive excitement of the world.

I pray I reflect the life of Lady.

Healing

They tell me
the hole in my heart
will heal.

Keep busy, they say.
Read a book.
Write a poem.
Go shopping.
Visit a friend.

These things
done many times over
do not reach my heart.

The double loss
lies too deep.

Falling Stars

When I reflect on my sixtieth year, I want to remember peering through the lens of a camera while hiking the circumference of Ireland; holding hands with Rubin in the cockpit of our sailboat, listening to the calls of loons echoing across the waters of the North Channel; launching a new website, blog, and pen name. I want to remember Rubin's dad squeezing my hand as Rubin and I sat with him before he died; the many months of quality time with Mother; my dad's trembling jaw as he whispered, "I love you, Mary."

I want to erase memories darkened by the brokenness of both our fathers' frequent falls, the cruelty of dementia in my dad, Parkinson's in my father-in-law, the lines of stress and exhaustion on our mothers' faces, and the quiet emptiness of death. I long to frame 2012 with treasures, not sorrows. But how?

Staring at the Arizona sky, I silently watch the stars twinkling overhead. Suddenly, without warning, they begin plummeting to the earth, so many points of light falling so quickly I cannot repeat my wish fast enough. It is as if the stars are reminding me that I am not alone and that an infinite number of angels are waiting for me to ask for help, waiting to make my wish come true.

Finding the Way

As we step out the door
for our morning walk
I ask: Which way shall we go?

Up the hill where desert wilderness
displays prickly pear and teddy bear cacti,
mesquite and palo verde trees?
Where rabbits scamper through the brush
and bobcats wait for their chance to pounce?

Or shall we go down the hill
to the shimmering lake
where fish poke their heads up for insects,
ducks cross the water in unison
and a heron swoops down
from a housetop across the road?

Which way shall we go?

There is no answer.
Lady, who always decided our route,
is no longer with me.

I walk up the hill alone.

Fear

"*Make yourself look large.*" I glance at my 5'5" frame, a body shaped by the lingering longings of an anorexic adolescence.

"*Stand your ground. Do not run.*" But I am a runner. It is what I do best.

"*Wave your arms. Shout. Throw rocks.*" Throw rocks? If survival depends on my throwing arm, I will be ripped apart before the first stone touches the desert sand.

"*This trail is closed.*" The somber park ranger points to the Three Tank Trail, a trail dangerously close to the one I've highlighted on the map of the Saguaro National Park Rincon Mountain District. "*It is where the mountain lion was sighted two days ago.*"

A tinge of doubt clouds my resolve to hike every mountain framing Tucson's skyline. I do not know what I am seeking as I don my worn, familiar hiking boots and loop the camera around my neck. Only that nature has always been my source of nourishment and I am suffering. And while a shortage of winter rains and several nights of bone-chilling frost have erased any hint of early spring wildflowers, I am excited about photographing a forest of the nation's largest cacti.

That was before learning that the 150-pound carnivorous cat which devours mule deer, elk, wild horses, domestic cattle, and prey much larger than me was seen demonstrating unusually aggressive behavior thirty-six hours earlier.

The emptiness of the trailhead parking lot stirs a queasiness in my stomach. The picture of the mountain lion stapled to a sawhorse with a bold-lettered sign announcing the trail closing adds to my uneasiness. I remind myself the route I've selected is considered safe, that it winds through a forest of giant saguaros, not the mountainous terrain of the cougars. Yet, I can't help but wonder . . .

Has anyone told the mountain lion to remain on the Three Tank Trail?

My aloneness is as stark as the mountains edged against turquoise skies. My feet drag along a path of saguaros towering thirty to forty feet overhead, many over 150 years old with multiple arms stretching to the sky. Vertical, needle-lined pleats define their skin and most are riddled with holes drilled by the Gila woodpecker or the gilded flicker. And yet, I see neither. I scour the skies looking for birds. Nothing.

My camera hangs limply around my neck.

I hike past a saguaro whose tip is crowned with a fan-like form, a rare and unexplained phenomenon of nature. I notice but do not lift the camera, blind to all save the imaginary shadow of the cougar stalking, waiting to pounce and dig sharp teeth into the soft skin of my neck.

I spin circles every couple hundred feet, checking my backside. But what would I do? What could I do? Fear, that deadly aroma that attracts predators, oozes from my pores. Only when the car is in sight and I pause to turn one last time do I notice an army of sparrows merrily flitting about the scrubby creosote bush.

On the way to Mother's house, I stop and purchase a whistle. I will not live with fear as my companion. But a whistle will not silence the trepidation tiptoeing toward my not-too-distant future. How do I walk alongside Mother as she heals when my home is so far away?

Ash Monday

I cannot be there
        so do not feel
                the frigid Michigan air.

Here, I am alone
        in the warmth
                of the morning sun.

I picture
        the loving hands
                of my Michigan family.

Placing ashes of my husband and Lady
        in a single niche
                among the evergreens.

Watching Another Suffer

I have knelt before a crucifix
  seeking answers, humbled
    by the mystery of understanding
      nothing.

I have curled my toes in the sand,
  and heard in the waves
    the sweetness
      of a lullaby.

I have tucked my head
  on another's shoulder
    and felt the peace that comes
      from acceptance.

So many choices
  on those days of trudging,
    why then are there times
      I can find nothing?

Boxes

Last year I didn't even think of them.

This year—two weeks before Christmas—
I suddenly remember they are on the top shelf of
the storage closet in the garage.

Do I drag the heavy boxes
down from their resting place?
Do I open each box?
Examine each item?
Choose what to display throughout the house?
And outdoors?

How can I do that?

He is not here to get the boxes down for me.
He is not here to fix himself a cup of coffee
and watch with a grin as I excitedly
pull the items out of the boxes one by one.
He is not here to help me make choices,
decide what to discard,
what to put back inside a box,
how to bring Christmas to our home.

He is not here and I cannot do that.

But I will buy two bright red poinsettias,
one for the living room,
the other for the kitchen-family room area.

I will smile and wish Merry Christmas
to all who enter my house.

The Day the Desert Rejoices

When one pauses to notice the mockingbird spinning cartwheels above his throne atop the palo verde; when one hears the deep-throated gurgle of a cactus wren, the high-pitched call of the Gila woodpecker, the mournful song of a lonely roadrunner, or the rapturous serenade of a curve-billed thrasher, the desert rejoices. The moment one sniffs the honey-like fragrance of the brownfoot and spots the tangerine color of the rare desert mariposa, the fire-orange tips of the ocotillo, the golden sunlight of a desert marigold, or the wispy pink petals of a fairy duster, the desert races to shower the prickly thorns of winter with its boldest splashes of spring. And when mother and daughter don walking shoes, brimmed hats, sunglasses, and hiking sticks to wander paved paths or sandy trails arm-in-arm, never have the birds chattered with such enthusiasm, the bees hummed with more vigor, or the flowers beamed with such exuberance as on that day.

The Concert

On my morning walk
I see a small brown sparrow
sitting on top of a bush
just my height.

I come so close
I could reach out
and touch him.
But I don't.

I look at him.
He looks at me.
Our eyes lock.
He begins to sing.

Joyous, lilting music
like I've never heard before.
I wish he would never stop.
But he does.

"Thank you, Bird," I whisper
as he flies away.
I continue my walk.
With a full heart.

Door Without a Lock

I waited by the phone for months,
hoping for a call, a text, anything
but the ongoing silence.

I stood in the doorway of hope,
arms extended, until
I could wait no longer

and had to walk ... jog ... run
into the hushed pink of dawn, leaving
the memories of our childhood footprints

behind. For a long time, I left the door
ajar, willing to suffer the reminder
of your rejection. Until I asked myself,

why? and closed the door and moved on.

Deep in My Heart

I wanted to see it
one last time—
the house that
had been home
to Harry, Lady and me.

The empty house echoes
with our steps
as Mary and I
carry the memory of
Harry and Lady with us
from room to room.

It goes with us
out the front door
where a group of neighbors
have gathered
with chairs
and treats
to bid me farewell.

It is a memory
I carry
deep in my heart.

Losses

Death, certainly, is the most permanent.
Like the time my older sister lost her kitten
to the teeth of the dog next door.

Or the morning he, who could no longer speak,
said goodbye to his wife with his eyes.
But I also have wept after witnessing

the mental and physical decline of ones I love;
at knowing I, too, am aging and life changes
are inevitable. I have experienced the betrayal

associated with harassment, discrimination, assault,
and the resulting loss of faith in humanity.
I am living with the heartbreak of seeing

the blue waters of a beloved lake blanketed green;
the sandy beaches I used to walk defined by pebbles,
impassable because of new rock embankments.

But the losses hardest for me to shoulder
are those caused by my own mistakes; when I,
usually speeding through life's to-do list,

trample on ones I care for deeply;
when I harm and am erased from a life,
a wall created to keep me outside.

How I deal with loss is a matter of choice.
And since all losses can potentially tear apart
any peace of mind, I want to choose wisely.

I asked my husband his thoughts
and he was surprised I cared so much
about football.

Michigan

The World I Left Behind

When I moved to Michigan
from my home in Arizona
I left behind . . .

Dozens of house sparrows
chattering in the pyracantha bush
growing against my back wall . . .

Fish bobbing to the surface
of the golf course water hole
to snap up unsuspecting insects . . .

Rabbits scurrying after one another
going from nowhere to nowhere
around the neighborhood . . .

Coyotes crossing the road from
one "wild woods" to the other
hunting their prey . . .

Spectacular orange colors
of every shade spreading across
the western sky at sunset . . .

But most of all the people,
the many wonderful friends—
loving and dear to me.

While I left all this behind
everything and everyone
stays vividly present in my memory.

Desert to Wetlands

"This apartment looks just like your mother," Rubin said the moment he opened the door and we saw the November sun flooding the living room with warmth.

Two years after the death of Dad and Lady, Mother decided to leave her home in Arizona so she could live closer to family. With six children scattered across the eastern part of the country, she selected Michigan, the place she and the family had lived for over thirty years, the state her two oldest daughters call home.

We thought it would be an easy search as Mother's requirements were minimal. She no longer wanted to cook meals, wanted a nice facility that was affordable and prohibited smoking, and wanted to be close to one of us. For weeks, Rubin, my sister and I scoured independent retirement facilities in the greater East Lansing area, the family's former home. Nothing. We searched the Holland area, Rubin and my hometown. Nothing.

I was on the edge of despair when a friend suggested a new building in one of Holland's senior living communities, roughly seven miles east of our house. Only one apartment remained available on the ground floor. With windows overlooking wetlands alive with the chatter of red-winged blackbirds, the quacking of ducks, the excited song of robins and wrens, Rubin was right. The apartment was perfect.

Mother was eighty-eight when she traded the sunshine of Arizona for the chillier days of Michigan. She says she has never regretted the decision. And while her presence altered my life and Rubin's, we agree. She is the oak tree in our lives. Resilient. Welcoming. A source of unconditional love that nourishes. When my confidence wanes, which it does frequently, she tells me she has plenty. "Just hang on to me," she suggests. And I will. As long as I can.

Outside My Window

Splotches of color
are sprinkled among
many shades of green.

Majestic trees
with emerald green leaves
sway gently in the whispering wind.

Deep green sunflower bushes
with brilliant yellow blossoms
lighten the far side of the pond.

Vivid purple wildflowers
growing in front of the pond
add color to old and faded plants.

Along the side of the pond
bright green cattails
wave in the wind as one.

In the background
bells from a nearby church
proclaim this holy ground.

Autumn Leaves

I never thought about wildflowers, never noticed them. I was too busy trying to balance my life as wife, daughter, sister and friend while working as a president within Baxter International. My calendar crammed with priorities, as I jogged in the early light of dawn I ignored the voice whispering to me to slow down, replenish, re-examine my life.

One day I decided to listen, to walk away from a thirty-year career. The only certainty I had was the overwhelming need to live near the eastern shores of Lake Michigan. When I closed my eyes to envision my future, I saw sparkling blue water stretching to infinity, heard the roar of waves pounding the beach, felt my feet sink into sand stretching from dunes towering overhead to water's edge, smelled the freshness of pines. My husband and I lived in Nashville, Tennessee, at the time. Our neighbors thought we were crazy. "People don't move north for the second half of their lives!" we were told repeatedly. But we had travelled extensively in our jobs, were fortunate to be able to live anywhere. Avid sailors who had sailed three of the five Great Lakes, we moved to west Michigan to live in the place of our dreams.

Life's transitions, I once read, are like the trees. In the autumn months, the leaves fall to the ground. No matter how much we'd like to replace them on the branches overhead, they remain on the earth's floor. We cannot go back. Winter follows, with its cold, gray days of deep soul-searching, painful self-examination. Difficult but necessary for spring to finally unfold.

I struggled after leaving Baxter. It's not that I wanted to return the leaves to the trees. I knew my life's purpose lay elsewhere. But where?

"What does your heart want?" a friend asked me. As I pondered her question in my early morning run the next day, the answer was immediate, but shocking.

"To go camping."

At the time, I had not camped since youth, so gear was nonexistent. But I decided to scrape together what I could find and set off alone to discover the dunes . . . and myself. The year was 2008. I was fifty-five. I set off in April. April in Tennessee is spring; April in Michigan, I was to learn, is borderline arctic.

Although the campsites were empty, as were the branches on the bushes and trees encircling my tent, I discovered I was never alone. Peeking through the remnants of winter—even that first week of April in the Indiana Dunes—were wildflowers.

How could I not greet them by name?

I began photographing them on hikes and looking through books in the evening next to a campfire to learn their names. I quickly discovered I needed to photograph all aspects of the flower, the blossom, stem, leaves—which meant I was often crawling along the earth's floor, photographing their intricate details.

The flowers, in turn, seemed to whisper the music of my heart. I began writing prose poems about the flowers, each written in exactly one hundred words. In hindsight, the self-imposed one-hundred-word mandate bridged a thirty-year career focused on analytical, left-brained activities and this new heartfelt voice unleashed by the discovery of nature's tiny treasures.

From the Indiana Dunes to Sleeping Bear, wildflowers dusted off the right side of my brain, the side that takes photographs, that writes poetry. The side that reminds me of my mother.

Trappings

My mind wanders incessantly as I tramp through the rolling hills.

"What will I do? What is my value? Who am I?"

Void of title, I am like a tiny grain of sand, easy prey for wind's fickle moods.

The endangered pitcher's thistle silences my chatter. Scrappy silver arms stretch across the dry sand. No giant leaves. No colorful petals. No excess. A pink smile of contentment touches her face.

Perhaps value is not defined by external trappings.

I pause to reflect on a message as rare as her smile and notice the sandpiper pecking furiously in the nearby water.

The Bribe

It was my mother who introduced me to poetry, gifting me *A Child's Garden of Verses* by Robert Louis Stevenson when I stood no taller than the kitchen table. The book was a bribe to entice me to quit sucking my thumb. The bribe didn't work, but the poems created the fabric of dreams, dreams placed on hold while I climbed the corporate ladder. When I learned that Lake Michigan and all the Great Lakes were at risk, potentially damaged beyond repair, I replaced my briefcase with a notepad and camera to help build the political will necessary to clean up and protect the lakes. The journey led me back to poetry, to a language with the power to influence how we treat ourselves, each other, the planet; a language that led me back to Mother.

Dealing with Loneliness

I often claim,
somewhat smugly,
that when loneliness hits me
I will deal with it.

So, now I admit
sometimes there is
an emptiness in my thoughts
and an aching in my heart
that distinguishes loneliness.

How do I deal with it?

I think about it for a while
suffering the aching and emptiness.
To me, it's important
to admit these feelings
and not pretend they don't exist.

Then I deliberately pull up
thoughts of people, things, activities
that bring great joy to me:
my family, close friends,
the place where I live—
with pond, ducks and trees in back—
the people living here,
walks to favorite spots,
reading Mary Oliver.

Thinking this way
causes me to feel
so fortunate
that my aches and emptiness
disappear.

Beauty in Imperfection

At first, I pay little attention as I trudge through the sand, intent on reaching the dune's summit. For I am a climber, trained to persevere, determined to conquer the mountain and view the world above the clouds.

Old habits die hard. But I am learning.

And so I hear her hushed cry. Retracing my steps, I kneel before her, photographing her wilting petals, pink with age and striped with the lime green of a virus.

"There is beauty in imperfection," I whisper to the trillium in her final moments on this earth.

And to myself, I repeat it constantly.

Mother's Day

Kathy—Mary—Tom
Karen—John—Helen

As I write the name
of each of my six children
my heart swells with
love, admiration, thanksgiving.

Each one of the six children
has a special place
in my heart.
Together they fill my life
with happiness.

Thank you, God,
that I am a mother.

Nature's Encore

It would take three of me, arms outstretched, to hug the girth of a gnarly cedar marking the entrance to Giants' Valley. In the shadows, troupes of floppy white trilliums gather, dancing wildly, celebrating spring.

Hiking quickly, I barely notice.

Shyly peeking her head from beneath a wide, green umbrella, the bell-shaped face of the nodding trillium stops me.

"What is your hurry?"

Embarrassed, I kneel to photograph the graceful bodies performing to the music of the southwesterly winds. As if in appreciation, the rare face of a red trillium peers around a downed giant, smiling for the camera.

A Soothing Peace

I was awakened
from my nap
by a steady tap-tapping
on my window.

It was rain—
a gentle rain
covering the world
outside my window.

The pond sang
a steady, happy tune
as the raindrops joined
the waiting drops within.

The tall, swaying trees
reached high into the sky
to grab every drop
of the much-needed drink.

The drooping cattails
stretched out their stalks
to catch the rain
and became instantly straight.

As for me—
I saw the gentle rain falling
and a soothing peace
flowed through me.

Playful Duck

Where is that duck?
He's playing
"hide and seek" with me.
He was here
and then he wasn't.

The sun
floods the pond
with brightness
and the duck
should be
enjoying it.
But where is he?

Just as I'm
about to give up
he pokes his head
out of the cattails—
and with him
comes another duck.

They swim around
in a small circle
one following the other,
then fly high in the sky
and out of sight.
I hope they remember
that this is "home."

Pioneer

It comes naturally to her. The sincerity. The softness. The
inclusive temperament. The quiet listening that draws others to
her. She can write. Knows how to ask questions. Is a natural in
front of the camera. As a result, when cable television became
widespread in the 1970s and the industry offered school districts
access, Mother, the Director of Public Information for the East
Lansing School District, jumped at the chance to use television to
bring the schools and community closer together.

It seems obvious now, interviewing the Superintendent of
Schools every Monday morning to discuss new ideas or respond
to concerns voiced by parents, teachers, students. She chose not
to share the questions in advance so the program had authenticity,
bridged the office with the public whose funding was necessary to
create a top-ranked school district. She invited English/Theatre
teacher Kate Veihl to join her so that high school students could
be involved in the production of the program and the creation of
a 24-hour school news channel—so that the students could learn
this new, unfamiliar technology.

Mother won national awards for her pioneering leadership
with this new medium, just one of many accolades she received for
her ability to combine her talents with her passion for ensuring
the public was informed, engaged and supportive of community-
wide education. In the eighteen years Mother was the Director of
Public Information, the millage passed every time it was on the
ballot.

So much I could have learned about leadership had I paused
and paid more attention instead of crashing, painfully, through the
glass ceilings of corporate life. So much I still can learn. On good
days. And bad. For aging gracefully is a new frontier for us both.

MOTHER

The Wanderer

The official name
of the plant is
sun parasol.
We call it The Wanderer
because its small branches
stretch out
in every direction.

The plant hangs
above the fence
in back of my apartment.
I admire it out the window
when I sit in my
bedroom recliner.

It is described in many terms:
easy care, large flowers,
vigorous growing climber,
excellent heat tolerance.

All that is true,
but the attraction to me
is that it is lovely to look at.

Lady-Two

Lady-Two has become one
of my all-time favorite "pets."

She has tan, fluffy, soft fur.
Her big, black eyes are both
loving and all-knowing.
And very real looking.

It was a special day
when daughter Mary
came into my bedroom,
where I was resting,
with the big, beautiful
stuffed puppy
filling her arms.

I instantly named her
Lady-Two
because of her resemblance
to long gone, much loved
Lady-One.

The Swallowtail Speaks to the Poet

I, too, was afraid
to leave the comfort
of the cocoon, to emerge
from the safety
of the shadows.
But having discovered
sunlight, I
soar dreamily
among the sweet-smelling
blossoms of the lilac,
flitting from one joyful
moment to the next.

My life is too short
to compare my resilience
to that of the monarch,
or worry the moth might
be lighter, nimbler
as it flutters through
a hedge of hydrangeas.
Instead, I spend each
sunlit moment sampling
the sweetness of the flowers,
delighting in the diversity
of earth's many gardens,
grateful I flew away
from the darkness.

They Come to Me

In the night they come to me
to envelope me in love
to whisper in my ear
they miss me
and are looking forward
to the time when I will join them.

In the night they come to me
to whisk away any worry
I might have
whether big or small
to assure me
I need have no concerns.

In the night they come to me.

A Bird Visit

He flew into
the tree
right outside
my window.

He had a
bright red streak
across his
black body.

He sang a
little song
then flew
away.

It was only
a few minutes
but it brought me
great joy.

Call of the Red-Winged Blackbird

I almost step
into the familiar fog
of inferiority
until I remember
to take the step
I don't want to take
and admit
I am good enough
to peer through the blinds
at the snow-capped cattails
inhaling the crispness
of the moon
good enough
to be in their presence
good enough to step
into the hush
of winter
and add my voice
to those who will
announce the dawn
knowing I must
take that first step
before I can take
the second.

Spring Snow

It's April. It's Spring.
Yet outside my window
tiny snowflakes
are coming straight down
thick and fast like rain.

Already there's a white
layer over the branches
on the small tree
close to my window.
The tall trees beside the pond
behind my building
are becoming invisible as I watch.

I suppose there are those
who resent this snowfall.
After all it IS Spring.
But the snow is beautiful.
If I were a child
I'd throw on my coat
and race outside
to make snowballs
and maybe
even a snowman.

As it is
I'll go to my recliner
and admire the falling snow
through the window.

Voice of Mother Goose

I hear him tell you from your porch, I am an aberration.
The pond is too small, the ledge too narrow.
Your daughter tells you I must be a first-time mom
and nicknames me "Abby" for short.

I watch you watch me, your eyes peering
from behind mullioned windows.
You, in your recliner, me scurrying about,
gathering the long-leafed remains of autumn.

I hear you greet me by name each morning,
tell me you, too, are a mom,
and that life as a mom is not easy, but worth it.
And then you wait, as do I, for the eggs. Six in all.

His words, which concern you, terrify me.
I don't know or care about that aberration thing,
but what was he saying about the pond? the ledge?
I pluck nervously at the nearby vegetation.
I don't know what else to do.

And then the rains begin battering my body.
And then snow. And hail. And then, more rain.
I tuck my face into fluffed-up feathers,
only my neck exposed. Week after miserable week.

You stay by the window, watching, whispering,
telling me to be strong, that they will hatch soon,
for my mate has returned and is circling nearby.
I hear but do not see you. I have eyes only
for the water inching higher.

...

There is no light in your room the night the winds
wage war on the pond. You do not see the waves
swamping my nest, or witness my life's work tumbling
into the frigid darkness. You do not see me fail.

Will you remember me? Come find me
on the high, grassy banks alongside the river?
I want you to know I will try again.
I suspect it's what you'd do, too.[1]

---

1 Note from daughter: This persona poem is based on a true story as
   witnessed outside Mother's bedroom window. I have read that the nest
   of the endangered piping plover met a similar fate on the shores of Lake
   Michigan, north of Chicago. It is a reminder that the consequences
   of climate change—to include the increasing number and intensity of
   storms—affects all life.

MOTHER

Lost Sun

Oh, bright, golden sun,
where are you?
The trees beside the sunken pond
stretch their barren limbs
to search the sky for you.
The cattails in the field
bow their heads in sorrow
at your absence.
The purple wildflowers
beneath my window
fold their petals in resignation.
I feel cold and alone
when you are not here
to lighten the sky.
Oh, bright, golden sun,
where are you?

The Guardian

Scout guards my back door.
He looks to the right;
he twirls to the left;
he swings in a circle
searching for anything
that looks suspicious.

If he wants my attention
he sounds the chimes
hanging below him.
If the sound is desperate—
like it might be an emergency—
I come running.

And there he is—
a metallic beauty—
Scout, the guardian
and happy hummingbird.

After She Tells Me She Loves Her Honda

Mother: I remember Rubin and I walking through row after row of cars in a large sales lot. He pointed out the differences in each car. He was very patient with me. Even though I no longer drive, I am grateful to have the car for my children to use when they visit.

Daughter: You always make the tough decisions. Not to drive. To move to Michigan. To turn your checkbook over to an accountant.

Mother: Actually, I don't like to drive. It's a big responsibility, particularly in a new place. And I like doing things with you and the other kids when they are in town—having my children drive me is much more fun than going alone. Even though the bulk of the responsibility now falls on your shoulders, you never make me feel like I am a burden. That's so important. You make everything an adventure. Even the grueling tasks of going to the doctor or the dentist.

Daughter: We are a team. And team members take care of each other.

Mother: I sure picked a good teammate.

Daughter: I was raised by the best.

Row of Red

Small green trees
lining the street where I live
are suddenly bright red.

The towering trees
along the street
around the corner
are turning gold.

The water in the lake
at the end of the road
is now dark, rich blue.

The trees and lake
are still beautiful.
But now they look
entirely different.

The magic of autumn
has touched them.

My Birthday

It is the first thing
that came to mind
when I woke up
this morning.

I am eighty-nine years old today.
I don't know
how you're supposed to feel
when you reach that age
but I know I don't feel
any different today
than I did yesterday.

So, I'll just go about
my usual day's activities.
The first thing is
thirty minutes of exercise.
They don't seem
any more difficult today
than yesterday.

After a breakfast of
oatmeal and muffin
I straighten up the house
then get to the computer
to work on my writing.
I will stick with that
for most of the day.

This is much like
every other day.

...

However, I think
next year will be different.
I'll make it so.
After all, reaching ninety
calls for celebrating
with my twin brother.

Sunset

One day last week
a group of residents
from my building
rode on a bus
to the state park
to watch the sunset.

We sat on benches
in front of a small
park supply building
a safe distance
from the water.
We were the only
people there.

Directly in front of us
the sun rested on
a light gray cloud
in the vivid blue sky
waiting patiently for us
to get settled so it could
complete setting.

We exclaimed loudly
about the miracle
happening in front of us—
and then the sun disappeared.
We had only the blue sky
and the still water
to admire.

To Somebody's Father

A block away and still I notice your tousled hair,
rumpled overcoat too small to button, eyes riveted
on me. Seven decades of training chill the sweat

off my body and yet I continue jogging toward you,
a compass needle drawn to the magnetic meridian.
But imaginary you are not and my head automatically

turns to avoid eye contact, the palm of my hand raised,
a shield as I pass. I say "no" before I can decipher
your words. I was raised to not speak to strangers.

The map in your hand stops me two strides past.
My dad purchased a new Road Atlas every year,
a book of dreams with Northwest pages dog-eared

and stained by hopeful hands. You tell me you are eighty-six,
one year younger than dad when death erased all roads
to Oregon and Washington. Visiting from Illinois,

you are searching for your son without car or suitcase,
just a downtown map, useless in neighborhoods.
Beneath your coat, your Sunday-best, but missing

are dentures that belong with that smile.
Yes, your son knows you are coming. No,
he is at work. No, they took your phone away.

We walk south, a straight line in a conversation
that zigs and zags like backroads through the mountains.
From an inside pocket, you pull your license.

It bears the same address as your son and I ask
if it would be okay if we wait together
at the corner for the patrol car.

Before climbing into the back seat,
you turn and shake my hand. I suspect
you are tired, ready to go home,

like the day my dad placed the Atlas
on the shelf, rather than next to his chair.

New Slogan

I have a new slogan.
It came about
because I moved too fast.

It's a trait I admit to:
>Hurry! Hurry! Hurry!
>Get where you're going *fast*!
>Don't fiddle-faddle!

So—true to my nature
I jumped up from the couch *fast*.
I was going to get a drink of water
but I changed my mind
and turned around very quickly.
Too quickly!
Wham!

As I fell to the floor
I caught myself with my hand
and sprained my wrist.
All because I moved too fast.

So, now my new slogan:
>*Go Pokey!*

She Knew Just What to Say

She knew just what to say
when the unexpected news
about my husband's heart
shook the cornerstones of my own.

"I am so sorry,"

said the woman who lost her dad
when she was eleven,
her husband and dog
within six weeks of each other,
who has shouldered the heartbreak
of illnesses and deaths
throughout her ninety-plus years.

"How are you doing?"

she asked, for she knows me,
can peel back the mask,
the false veneer of stone,
can see the seeds of anxiety
racing through me
like a rain-swollen river.

"What can I do to help you?"

she offered, for despite her experience,
perhaps because of it, she does not
make suggestions, for she knows
her path may not
be the right one for me.

· · ·

"I will pray for you."

she said, for she has prayed
for me, and with me,
since she first heard
my heartbeat within her,
long before I knew
words could be so powerful.

Problems

All my adult life
I have been able
to put a problem
I cannot solve
into a box
and set it aside
out of sight and
out of mind.

Now, at ninety-one years old
I find I am
not able to do that.
Problems I cannot solve
I must learn
to live with.

I pray a good deal.

Magical Moment

When John Dennis was
visiting me several years
ago, we went to
Windmill Island
so he could see
The Windmill.

The park was closed
as it was winter.
But we could see
The Windmill from
the parking lot.

As I pointed it
out to John Dennis
The Windmill slowly
turned its blades.

I had never seen
this happen before.
Nor had I ever
heard of anyone else
seeing it!

The Windmill turned
its blades for
my twin brother.

The Sun

Oh, bright, golden sun
    there you are!
The trees beside the glowing pond
    stretch their leaf-covered arms
    in thanksgiving for you.
The cattails in the field
    hold high their heads in joy
    at your presence.
The purple wildflowers
    beneath my window
    unfold their petals in celebration.
I feel warm and soothed
    when you are here
    to lighten the sky.
Oh, bright, golden sun
    there you are!

The Pandemic

The Poet Speaks to the Swallowtail

You did not warn me about storms,
how each drop of rain is like
a bowling ball battering your body;
how the slightest decline in temperature
can send you spiraling to the earth's floor
where hungry beaks and sucking mouths
anxiously await your floundering arrival.

I did not see you slip quietly into the brush
when thunder roared in the distance;
how tightly you folded your wings
to rest and wait for the storm to pass.
I saw only joy-filled flights through
a sun-flecked garden, never realizing
what was necessary to survive.

Winter Reigns

The sun shines
high in the sky
spreading its warmth below
as though it might be spring.

The trees, though leafless,
glitter in the sun
like they might turn green
at any moment.

The pond, though icy,
glimmers brightly,
as its surface mirrors
the brilliance of the sun.

I look out my window
and yearn to rush outdoors
to bask in the sun's
soothing warmth.

But the trees, pond, and I
know the sun is fooling me.
Winter reigns
and spring is far away.

Prayer for the Caregivers

Just before Easter weekend of 2020, Rubin and I said goodbye to his mother as she slipped away from us, alone in a hospital bed in Midland, Michigan. A nurse just off her shift provided the phone that made those tearful goodbyes possible.

Irene was not a victim of COVID-19, but certainly a casualty of the rules necessary to keep us safe. At roughly the same time Michigan was locked down because of the coronavirus, Irene fell and shattered her hip. Ninety-one years of age, she faced an uphill recovery in a rehabilitation hospital, a journey made more difficult without the presence of family and friends.

Before the rapid decline that necessitated a transfer from the rehabilitation hospital to the ER, caregivers took their own phones and tablets to Irene's bedside so she could Skype with her children. For over a week, the family laughed and shared stories together as if we were around her kitchen table.

Many have similar stories before a vaccine was developed to help keep us safe, before we were able to hold the hand of a loved one suffering in a hospital, rehabilitation or nursing home bed. But during the height of the pandemic, we depended on physicians, nurses and aides to provide bedside emotional support as well as physical care; especially the aides—the caregivers who bathed, dressed, changed, and responded to the call buttons of the sick, the elderly, the dying.

Irene passed early Easter morning. And while prayers flow easily from my heart these days, at the top of the list is a prayer for those who made it possible for Irene to know she was not alone.

Her Heart Was in the Sugar

For Irene Schmidt, 5/10/1928-4/12/2020

It would be heavenly if she could see
her children on the front yard again,
glance at them through the window
above the sink as she fills the house

with the sweet smells of her baking;
if, when she called them for dinner
they came running, knowing what was
waiting in the oven after vegetables.

If only she again could use lard in her crusts,
ample sugar in her fillings. If only
she didn't have to worry about her health,
or theirs. She lies on the kitchen floor, staring

at the dark spot on the ceiling above the oven,
trying to ignore the pain slicing through her side.
How long ago was it? That day smoke filled
the kitchen? That day her children told her

to quit baking? That day everything changed?
She hears a strange voice calling her name,
asking if she is alright. Commotion in her entry.
Closing her eyes, she smells the fragrance

of a freshly baked pie, sees angels bounding
in her direction, notices God reaching toward her,
a dessert plate between thumb and forefinger,
and hopes she remembered to add enough sugar.

A Gray Day

Gray . . . everything is gray.
The sun is hiding
behind thick, dark clouds.
The small pond lies underneath
a thin layer of gray-brown mush.

Weeds and cattails,
suffering from their battle
with winter wind,
lay stricken around the edge
of the mud-matted pond.

Stick-like trees
reach high into the sky
begging for the sun
to cover them
with warmth and color.

I turn from the window
so the sight
of the gray outdoors
will not leave me
feeling gray inside.

Our Time

What a time this is!
Coronavirus has
settled over us
and changed our
world drastically.

People are directed
to stay home
except for emergencies.
Stores are closed.
Activities are cancelled.

For all that
    the sun is shining brightly,
    the ground outside my window
    is peppery green,
    large white blooms cover
    the magnolia bushes
    lining the building,
    two ducks are swimming
    in the pond,
    a peaceful stillness covers everything.

All this reminds me
no matter what goes on
in the world around us
we must accept it willingly
and remember God is in charge.

Why Toilet Paper?

I want to write a poem
about the fox or the robin
the turkeys or the moon
or even the radiant colors
of last evening's sunset
but all I can think about
are those empty store shelves
knowing at some point
I will get down to that last roll
and nowhere
in my boxes
of memorabilia
is there
a Sears catalog.

A Blank Mind

Written on my calendar for today is one word:

Write.

But I'm sitting here with pen and paper and a blank mind.

It's dark and dreary outside.
I don't want to bring it inside. So, I'm trying to think
of something cheerful
to write about.

However, my mind
is not cooperating. There is nothing
more frustrating
than trying to bring something to mind
when your mind is blank.

I will give up for now, take a little nap
then try to bring
my mind back to life.

The Wind

I never imagined
I would ever write
about the wind.
But today
it is demanding
my attention.

The wind is racing
around the side
of the building,
howling fiercely,
pushing aside everything
that gets in its way.

From the safety
of my living room window
I see a lawn chair
tumble off a nearby patio,
a bird feeder fly high
into the air.

The trees beside the pond
tip their branches
almost to the ground;
the water in the pond
rushes to cover
everything around it.

All this is done
with a violent fury,
a warning to

...

get out of the wind's way
or suffer its anger.

I heed its warning
and sink lower
into the safety and
comfort of my recliner.

Tilley Hat

Dining room. Closed.
Exercise room. Closed.
Activities suspended.
Visitors forbidden.
Masks mandatory.
No gathering in halls, foyers,
apartments. Especially apartments.
Rules designed to keep them safe
in effect indefinitely. Rules
residents do not understand. Or they forget.
Or, like a prowling cat at midnight,
choose to ignore.
How to keep her healthy
during this pandemic?
Physically active, upbeat,
mentally alert in such strict
but necessary isolation?
How do I keep Mother, Mother?

Rummaging through the closets
of my mind, I remember
a gift from her eldest son,
a white brimmed bucket hat,
perfect for outdoor adventures
into the world of the swans,
squirrels, sunflowers, geese,
cottonwoods, and swallows.
Week after week,
month after month,
we stroll through parks
observing, listening, discussing

...

all we might use to create
poems. I carry a camera
to record possibilities.
She wears a hat of freedom.

Peace and Tranquility

We call it
Cottonwood Corner.
Mary and I
claim a bench there
under the trees
beside Lake Macatawa.

We can view the beautiful lake
and enjoy the sense of
peace and tranquility
the lake provides.

Our "Corner" is made up
of seven immense
cottonwood trees growing very
close together in a row
beside the lake.

Our bench is the only
bench. We are surprised
no one else is around.

Surviving

Despite the garlic mustard
marching as an army across the dune,
or the herd of ever-grazing deer,
or the clawed paws of the squirrels
scampering from tree to tree,
this morning, among the crumbling leaves
of last year's memories, I discovered
a trillium, nudging me onward,
and on our front porch,
packages of toilet paper
from two of God's angels,
reminding me
we are not alone.

Unhappy Squirrel

After our walk along
the path beside
Lake Macatawa,
Mary and I decided
to rest on a bench
under the trees
beside the water.

We barely got
ourselves situated
when a squirrel
in the tree beside us
began to talk to us—
in a calm, peaceful
way at first.

But the longer
we sat there
the fiercer the
squirrel's tone
became.

We even felt an
acorn or two
come from the
squirrel's direction.
There was no missing
the squirrel's message—
it didn't want us there.

...

Finally, the squirrel
came racing down the tree trunk
and stood directly in front of us.
It made a short, ferocious speech
then scampered away.
It did not return.

DAUGHTER

The Breakfast Bench

Concealed by a family of Dutch immigrants
cast in bronze and framed in flashy hibiscus,
surrounded by black-buttoned gold called Susans,
a clumpy hedge of roses, a wall of waist-high grasses,

the bench, the two women agree
as they stroll up the cobbled path,
is perfect. Perched on top a grassy hill
overlooking a familiar lake,

steps from parking, ignored
by book clubbers seated in a circle
under the arms of an oak,
the knee-high toddler skipping

atop a wall, pregnant mom in chase,
the lovebirds cooing on a distant bench,
the faraway look of a man, fishing pole
leaning against the fence, line dangling,

the wooden bench is ideal for the daughter
and her mother searching for a place
to share the rare treat of fresh muffins,
discuss wind and water, ripples, cats' paws,

the speed and roar of powerboats,
the slow, deliberate journey of sailors.
When they return, autumn wafts
across the water. First, it is the elder

···

who is limping, an infection, arthritis;
then the younger, a sprain, a fracture.
The women agree the bench is perfect,
a short walk to normalcy; building winds,

the hum of boats, the cry of seagulls,
the parade of strollers along water's edge,
a conversation in the language of sailing
on a bench that has weathered the seasons.

The World Around Us

There is no sun in the sky.
There are no leaves on the trees.
The cattails are dirty brown
                    and scraggly.
The world around us is
                    dark and dreary.

            But
beneath my window
the ground shimmers
with thousands of
tiny, yellow blossoms
poking up from a carpet
of brilliant green.

            And
Suddenly it is OK
if the sun isn't shining
and there are no leaves
                    on the trees
and the cattails are
dirty-brown and grey.
The world around us is still
                    bright and beautiful.

Escaping Geese

We see the geese
when we go walking
on the path
along the river's edge.

They look stately
as they strut
beneath the trees.

Even though they are careful
not to come too close to us
my insides tremble
as though they are poised to attack us
at any minute.

The feeling goes back
to my younger days
as a Girl Scout leader.
I often took my girls
on a hike to the park.

On the way
we cut through
a vacant lot.
One day a flock
of geese surprised us.

I led the group of girls
racing as fast
as I could.

Luckily, the geese
didn't follow.

We never walked
through that vacant lot
again.

Learning Another Language

"…But Only God Can Make a Tree"
Joyce Kilmer

The orange-breasted birds greet us like old friends,
two women escaping the suffocating walls
of a lingering pandemic. Her one arm around mine,
we stroll through the park delighting

in the chirp of the cardinals,
the schizophrenic soaring of the swallows,
the dashing hop of the gray, black, and brown squirrels.

Once, from a distance, we saw a family of swans
and from then on, our walks took on new meaning
as we searched for the babies, cygnets, I'm told.
And once, when she thought she could go no further,

I urged her to peek around the corner, just in case,
and, sure enough, they were there. And we continued
to path's end to see the families of geese and ducks
tucked safely among the shadows of the trees.

II

Today, there are no robins, cardinals, chickadees,
or swallows. No squirrels. Only the rowdy winds
of autumn, roaring through a riverbank of stumps.
Raw, ravaged stumps.

In my mind, I am penning a letter to a city which chooses
to listen to those demanding a view, but doesn't ask us

who prioritize seeds, not chain saws; who recognize trees
as essential to addressing the climate challenges
facing the planet; who . . .

I stop because she has stopped, her eyes staring up
at the leafy arms of the sole remaining cottonwood,
and I hear from her lips a song as beautiful as any robin.
> *I think that I shall never see*
> *A poem lovely as a tree. . .*

My raging rant dissolves into the lyrics
of Kilmer's poem, recited by one
whose memory is fading; who,
in few words, says everything as she
spreads the world with honey.

An Unusual Gift

When we arrived at
the Breakfast Bench
Mary and I found
a lone woman sitting there.

So we settled for a backup bench
beside the walkway
along Lake Macatawa
where we could see the lake.
Unfortunately, the world
could view us, too.

This was no Breakfast Bench
which provides privacy,
comfort, and a perfect
view of the lake.

But we settled ourselves down
to enjoy this new scene.
Suddenly, a passing bird
dropped a gift for me—
a huge blop
right on my leg!

We couldn't help
but laugh
at this unusual gift.

DAUGHTER

Fourteen Days

There is no Ouija Board this time.
No high-pitched laughter among friends
slipping underneath a closed bedroom door.

No bodies fluid and flexible flung across
a young girl's bed or sitting cross-legged nearby.
No whispered talk of boys or proms, sex or marriage.

Just a daughter sitting on the edge of the bed,
phone in hand; a frightened doe caught
in the headlights. Her mother's earlier fall,

an ambulance, a crushed arm, ulcerated wound,
a surgeon's order to provide 24/7 care,
a suggestion for rehab, assisted living.

But memories scream a siren song.
Not again. Not the other parent.
Not against her will. No.

She asked the surgeon, if it was his mom
with the risk of COVID, mandated isolation,
chance of mental decline, what he'd do.

He said he'd try and keep her at home.
Which is exactly what she did. But
words over the phone pierce like bullets.

Nighttime caregiver tested positive.
Mother and daughter exposed. Shortage of tests.
Mandatory quarantine. Fourteen days

...

and nights. But no nighttime assistance.
No bathers. No wound clinic. No physical therapist.
Urgent trips every half hour to the smallest room

as an infection goes untreated, sample lost
in the crush of patients overwhelming
physicians in the autumn of 2020.

Roles reverse between mother and daughter
but nothing of substance changes.
Two women caring for each other,

nibbling on popcorn, watching funny movies,
making nickel bets on football scores,
calling it an extended slumber party.

He is Not Here

He is not here
to celebrate our
wedding anniversary—
to remember with me . . .

Standing beneath
a floral arch
promising to love
one another
till death do us part . . .

Being followed
as we leave
on our honeymoon
by my twin brother
and his buddies,
honking and yelling,
telling the world
we are newlyweds . . .

Eating our first dinner
in New Orleans—
climbing a ladder
to get to our table
in the top
of a tall, bushy tree.

He is not here
to remember
this day with me.
But I am filled

...

with tender thoughts
of my deceased love.

A Daughter's Thoughts on Compression Stockings

If these socks are the future of forty percent of the population,
a byproduct of aging veins that refuse to push blood
back to the heart but, instead, leave it pooling beneath
paper-thin skin waiting to erupt as an ulcerated wound

and become a feeding ground for deadly infections,
why were they manufactured to be as stubborn
as the flying squirrel scratching a home in her attic?

And, if she is to unroll these stockings of steel
from toe to ankle to knee without causing pain
and without leaving unsightly, potentially dangerous

rolls of fabric on the legs of her mother, why
weren't her fingers created to be as nimble and strong
as the raccoon ripping apart her freshly planted garden?

And, if there truly is a caring God, why is this stocking
she finally has muscled up the calf of the sympathetic
woman watching her struggle, inside-out?

Promise of Spring

Walking on the path
along the river
with the trees budding
and the birds singing
I am overcome
with the promise
of spring.

Everywhere there are "twos"—
the ducks in the water
the geese along the shore—
even birds in the trees
call eagerly to each other.

Sometimes, instead of "twos"
there are "threes"
or even "fours"
as little ones
follow along
behind the parents.

It is spring—
joy and promise
brighten the world.

No Leisurely Stroll

The man soldiers beneath an overstuffed backpack
towering above his head. Oblivious to the sultry
mid-morning sun, unaffected by sweat dribbling
down cheeks grayed by a closely cropped beard,

lost in sounds emanating from white earbuds,
he is not a familiar face encountered on my jogs;
not a walker, fellow runner, poop-picker-upper.
I pause mid-stride to raise a questioning eyebrow.

When I hear wilderness training, I remember
a forty-four-pound forest-green backpack that included
a Dutch oven so the girls could bake their first
pineapple upside-down cake over a campfire;

rain tarps to stretch between trees at night—
knowing on clear nights, we would inch our bags
from beneath the tarps to sleep under the stars.
And the moon. Especially the moon.

I remember difficult ascents up rocky trails,
finally reaching that place above the tree line
where the air was crisp and clouds floated below us;
where the earth seemed silent, peaceful, divine.

Such a long time ago.

Today, there is no pack on my shoulders
and yet sweat rolls in rivers down cheeks
the color of Ida's apples as I ponder my mortality,
my husband's, mother's, and the choices

...

that braid our lives together.
The hiker asks for what am I training,
and to his surprise and mine
I reply, *life.*

Where Are the Ducks?

I look out my window
and they are not in the pond.
Where are the ducks?
Where do they go
when they leave the pond
I call their home?

Have they found a pond
they like better?
Or have they decided
to join their many kin
always present on
nearby Lake Macatawa?

When I look out my window
and the ducks are not present
in the small pond
behind where I live,
I am filled with
a strange longing.

Conflict

Fueled by passion
I stormed through life
with good intentions
leaving
in my wake
silent resistance
until
something
or someone
gave me pause
something
or someone
suggested
another way
and sitting
in that moment
of stillness
I chose
differently
but you
were
already
gone.

Chair Chat

It's Spring

Everything is
green and growing
outside my window.

The trees
beside the pond
are no longer
tall, thin stalks
but bright green fans
waving in the wind.

The ground
beneath my window
is no longer
flat, brown dirt
but a green, leafy bed
with tiny, yellow blossoms.

The tall and stately
Berry-Bird tree
has small, red berries
growing thick
among the bright
green leaves.

I sit in my recliner
with Lady-Two
a stuffed, life-like retriever
from Mary
in my lap
admiring all

...

the new life
of spring.

DAUGHTER

Were It Not for the Moon

So many things to check off the list, the stuff of life that overwhelms, consumes, depletes. You know what I mean. I have lived my life defined by what I do, but there are moments too powerful to ignore, like the time the full moon edged its way through the blinds in Mother's bedroom as she slept in the recliner by the window. Her eyes were closed, yet her head was tilted to the skies, her expression one of wonder. It looked as if sometime in the night she heard the voice of God calling to her from that circle of light in the darkness. How could I not slide to the floor at her feet and wait for her to waken? How could I not change my priorities? And remember my name is Mary, not Martha?

Under a Bushel Basket

Daughter: She saw the seeds of an artist in me long before I did. I remember she took me across town every Saturday morning so I could participate in painting and drawing classes for children. I loved the classes, but even more, I loved my one-on-one time with her in the car.

Mother: I wanted to find special things I could do with each of my children. Things that would be meaningful to me and to them.

Daughter: And then she loaned me her manual black-and-white Smith-Corona so I could get the job at the weekly newspaper, and I discovered writing.

Mother: I was proud to have a daughter actually writing—to be able to share something that is such an important part of my life.

Daughter: But then I quit the newspaper, quit college and took off to Africa. That had to have been hard on her. I think of it as my rite of passage. I had no money, got a job for a couple of months as a waitress in Johannesburg and then took off in a crotchety white van with friends to explore the southern part of the continent. Of course, the van died and I found myself hitchhiking along the eastern coast of South Africa. When I returned to the states, I vowed I'd never be poor again. Shut down my artistic brain and focused on learning the skills of the business world, followed in the footsteps of my father.

Mother: Africa scared me to death. I had to put it out of my mind. She came back a different person. Hardened. Focused. Determined.

Daughter: I think it was my guardian angel who whispered in my ear thirty years later, who told me to change course, to pull my natural talents out from beneath the bushel basket from which they'd been buried. To return to writing. Take up photography. To combine the best in me from both parents. But natural talent is one thing; courage to share is something else. All that confidence I mustered while working for the newspaper, for Baxter, disappeared. I don't have a company name next to mine. It's just me. My mind. My heart. Me.

Mother: To be a writer is to have thick skin. One has to be tough. Get over caring what other people think. Be true to yourself and do your best. Eventually it will become enjoyable. Never easy. But fulfilling.

Daughter: It will be hard for me when she is not here.

Mother: I will always be with her. Especially when she is writing.

Daughter: I will always write.

Turquoise Plaid Pajamas

Will I remember how peaceful she looks tucked in the recliner, her comforter pulled up against her chin, the life-like golden retriever draped across her lap? How her head lists to the right as she sleeps? How delight sweeps across her face when she opens her eyes and I am there? How she raises her arms for a hug and her excitement is like a flock of robins feasting on the berries of a crabapple tree in winter? How anticipation, hers and mine, swirls about our shoulders as I slide down the side of the bed to the floor at her feet for our chat? How our conversation flows as a river, sometimes slow, sometimes fast, but always moving? How, when I help her rise from the recliner on the count of three, we pause for a morning embrace? How her hair tickles my nose as I kiss the top of her head? How the softness of her fleece pajamas breaks my heart open to the possibilities of each new day? How I left a note to the caregivers asking that Mother's pajamas be spared the whirling efficiency of the dryer? How I hoped air-drying would preserve the feel of the fleece?

The Blossom

She's loyal—
      Always there for me to admire
She's beautiful—
      Deep pinkish-purple—the only
      blossom on a tall, thick-leaf bush
She's available—
      Right outside my bedroom window
She's inspirational—
      I keep pen and paper handy

She doesn't have a name
      but that's OK.
She's just "The Blossom."

Miracle Within Small Things

It is how we begin every morning;
she in the recliner, me sliding down the bed
to the floor at her feet for our chairside chat.

But this morning, there is heightened excitement
in her voice and her mind is as alert as I've seen
in many months. It is not the snow-white blossoms

outside her window, the sight of the male mallard
creating circles on the pond, the animated chatter
of the robins, sparrows, and red-winged blackbirds,

the yellow flowers of the mock strawberries
dancing across the green carpet bordering
the beleaguered remnants of the cattails.

Contributors, certainly.
But this surprising, youthful exuberance
is the result of a decorative tree in a city park

with a bench that will soon be placed nearby.
On the bench, a plaque celebrating a poem,
her poem, and the lives of a pair of twins, intertwined.

Had I known the effect this simple request
would have on my mother, I would have cared more
about their decision and possibly ruined everything.

As it was, I let go and am watching a miracle unfold,
just like the pink buds on the small magnolia tree
we will visit this afternoon.

The Jane Tree

She stands alone—
but not one bit lonely—
in the middle
of a small, square yard
on Windmill Island.

She's not very tall—
I can almost touch
the topmost branch.
She has pinkish-white buds
that will soon burst forth
into snow-white blossoms.

There is a bench
at the back of the yard
where we can sit
and see the bridge and path
leading to The Windmill
and the constant stream
of people going there.[2]

---

2   The Jane Tree is one of eight hybrid magnolia cultivars known as "the
    girls": Magnolia Ann, Betty, Jane, Judy, Pinky, Randi, Ricki, Susan.

The 'Girl' on Windmill Island

Were it not for her name, we would have missed her.

Tens of thousands of eye-popping tulips, the unfamiliar music of the street organ, the Friesian horses in the field, the replica of the Dutch village, the romantic allure of the red and white bridge, and the winding path to the famous "De Zwann" windmill are overwhelming attractions. She is, after all, small in stature and tucked in a corner alongside the river. Without even a nearby bench to give one pause, to invite the weary to sit and smell the sweetness of her tulip-like blossoms, admire the glossy green leaves of summer, she lives alone. Unnoticed.

Her name is Jane.

Unlike the other seven hybrid magnolia trees in the family of "Little Girls," the Jane Tree was named after a wife, not a daughter. And not just any wife, Jane was named after the wife of Orville Freeman, the twenty-ninth governor of Minnesota, a Lutheran deacon who campaigned against religious bigotry and nominated the first Catholic president for office in 1960. He was a two-term Secretary of Agriculture who initiated the food stamp and school meal programs and was known for his focus on increasing farm incomes while using surpluses to feed the hungry.

The tree's history is as rich as that of the island.

Although ninety-four years old, Mother will put her arm in mine and walk the island to listen to the red-winged blackbirds, eye the ducks and geese and—once—the tundra swans, marvel at the butterflies and gardens, and, of course, visit the Jane Tree. While at the tree, we talk about family.

Mother, too, was named after an influential Democrat, Virginia Ellen Flood (1902-1985), her mother's sister. While details of her aunt's life are sketchy, we know she went by "Jane" and owned and managed one of the largest insurance agencies in Oklahoma in the middle of the 20th century. She was a trailblazer for women in business and politics before we understood what that meant.

Similar to her namesake, Mother is also considered a pioneer, but in education. Like the tree, the Janes in our family are strong, resilient. And they span multiple generations, three of whom posed with the Jane Tree in 2018, when the family held its seventieth consecutive annual family reunion—this one in Holland.

Thanks to the Windmill Island Garden Development Manager and the Rotary Club of Holland, the Jane Tree received its bench. As a result, visiting the tree, the bench and the small triangle of grass has become our favorite adventure. We call it the "Jane Tree Corner."

Legacies

The morning of the moon's passing,
she whispered the unthinkable—
that she had not the energy
to keep writing.
Like the tundra swans,
necks long and extended,
stretching to reach the Carolinas
from their home in the Arctic,
it was all she could do to get by.

And then she chanced upon a note
written to her from a legendary poet,
picked up a pen and wrote a poem.
And then another. And another.
And encouraged her daughter
to do the same. As she had
so many long miles ago.

For poet Jack Ridl

Special Plants

They are invasives—
the most hated ones—
the ones no one wants
growing in their gardens.

They thrive in ditches
along country roads.
On a Sunday drive
I saw them and cut a few
to put in vases
throughout my apartment.

Some are purple,
some white—
one even orange.
Some are large blooms,
some small.
All are beautiful.

They are called weeds.

On Bad Days

A drop of dew
dribbles
down a stem,
lingering slightly
on each tiny hair
before continuing
to earth's floor.

Gravity will not
be thwarted.
Nor will
the snowballing
effects
of time.

So, why
on days
is it so difficult
to find
the robin-egg blue
of the sky?

MOTHER

A Lost Boy

For John Dennis Laflin, 10/30/1926-11/16/2020

Standing by myself in the school hallway,
staring out the window,
hoping I can see him coming.
I can't.

Our first time walking alone
the six blocks from home to school.
At the corner I say: We turn.
He shakes his head and goes straight.

My six-year-old heart sinks to my toes.
Where can he be?
Tears slip down my cheeks.
He's lost in this new, big city.

I can't leave the window.
I can't stop the tears.
He's lost. It's all my fault.
I should have stayed with him.

I feel a touch on my shoulder.
The principal asks: What's wrong?
I stutter through the tears:
He's lost . . . he wouldn't turn . . . he's lost.

She leads me gently into her office,
wipes my tears, gives me a sip of water.
We'll find him, she assures me.
Don't worry. We'll find him.

...

They do.
The seventh-grade boys find him.
He comes slowly through the door.
I run to hug my twin brother.
Not in public, he whispers.

Resolution

The world is dark and flat.
Not even a tree to break the horizon.
No birds to sing through the silence.

She awakens, lost, alone, distraught,
unable to resolve this recurring
nightmare: the death of her twin.

I listen at her feet, longing to soothe
as she has soothed. For unlike her,
my night demons frequently

pierce me, leaving me wide-eyed
and staring at the numbers of a clock
until dawn.

There are things beyond my control—
illness, dementia, death.
I do not want her to suffer,

and so I begin . . .

"In your dream, look for the pinhole
of light among the clouds. Climb through it
and into the open arms waiting for you."

Me? I run to the meadow in the sun,
the one with the dancing wildflowers,
flop down in the tall grass among angels

and pray I will see her again.

Joy in My Heart

When my spirit is low
and my heart is heavy
I need only look
out my window
and suddenly my
spirit is lifted and
joy fills my heart.

The Wanderer on the fence
boasts multiple
bright red blossoms.

Close to my window
the hydrangea bush
is covered with blooms
of cream-colored fluff.

Above both fence
and hydrangea bush
the Berry-Bird tree displays
numerous tiny red berries.

To accompany all this
the birds in the trees
chitter-chat
their happiness.

Three-Letter Word

A red, green and white Christmas embroidery hangs
year-round in her living room. Long, narrow,
it spells out a word she says occasionally
as we slog through our daily exercise routine,

one written frequently, she tells me, in her journal,
a three-letter word to which I never gave thought
until now, when I am running out of time to learn.

Like the butterfly soaring for the first time
into summer skies, the hooked fish released
to dart again through the river of its home,
my mother lives with joy.

I want the same.

However, I can be my father's daughter
and worries fuel my sleepless nights;
perfection punctures success, and the suffering
of others shatters any hope for happiness.

Joy is as elusive as the red fox of the forest.

Outside her bedroom window, we watch
the robin, plump with eggs, flit between fence
and berries. The vines of a parasol plant,
leaves glossy, blossoms red and plentiful,

wander playfully in all directions. The pond
is disappearing, as are her beloved ducks,

...

but the encroaching cattails provide cover
for the families of serenading wrens

and rambunctious red-winged blackbirds.
So much for which to be grateful, she reminds me.

Family

I see the word
I hear the word
I think of the word—
any of the above—
and a gentle warmth
flows through me.

Add "my" to the word
and I think of "reunion."
My family has held
a family reunion every
June since 1948
until last year, 2021.
The reunion was
"postponed" because
of the pandemic.

That's reunions
every year for
seventy-two years!

My mother held
the first reunion
when she invited
her siblings and
children to
join her to celebrate
the safe return
of all the young
men in our families
from World War II.

...

The families decided
to meet again and
it evolved into
meeting every year.

Eventually, participants
narrowed down to my
mother's family—
as it has been ever since.

I feel so strongly about
family because
it gives me a
sense of security,
of belonging,
of being loved.

DAUGHTER

Have I Told You Enough?

The rumbling, though far in the distance, triggers
a quickening of my heart and I grip the paddle,
remembering when things did not go well,

when I was deceived by the glassy surface of the water
concealing the perils beneath the swift-flowing river;
when I smashed into the boulders, was thrown

into the roaring rapids, swallowed by haystacks
and sent tumbling downstream in the raging waters.
When it comes to love of any kind,

experience matters and memories float like a leaf alongside,
eroding confidence. One can paddle faster than the current,
or slower, but allowing the river control ensures defeat.

These days I dig the blade hard into the water behind me.

There have been times I opted to paddle
the safe waters of an inland lake, reveling
in the stillness as I lazily searched for a sandhill crane,

the checkerboard back of a loon, a tundra swan.
But most of the time it is the river that lures me,
and I have eyes only for the fast-flowing waters

and the image of you downstream,
looking for pebbles to polish.

Sign of Winter

The first bit of snow
is on the ground today—
not thick and solid—
just here and there.

But it is the first sign
that winter is here.
What does that mean to me?

I don't spend time
outside any more
so it shouldn't
matter to me
what's going on outside.

But it does!

When the Sun is shining
I'm alive and perky.
When it's dark and dreary
I slide under my afghan.

When I slink
under the afghan
I invariably reach
for pen and paper.

Like now!

Remembering

It has been several years but still
we remember and look
to the second-floor balcony
where he used to sit in a lawn chair
and wave to us when we returned;
how he used to save you a seat
at the dining table, back when they had staff
to serve dinner to interested residents;
how he shared with you the days, weeks, months
he once sat by his wife, holding the hand
of a woman who no longer recognized him,
and that he loved her still;
how he, too, had a daughter
who cared for him, much like I care for you,
how he kept falling until one day
his daughter thought it safer
if he moved across the street,
and he, reluctant to leave his friends
but not wanting to be a burden, agreed;
how the street made it feel
as if he was a continent away
so that we visited only twice
before the lockdown;
how one day we received a note
from his daughter that our friend, Jim,
had died from COVID;
how we wrote her a note
telling her how proud he was
she was his daughter;
how I wish we'd crossed that street
a few more times;

...

how you reminded me
we did the best we could.

Yesterday and Today

Yesterday, the sun covered
all outdoors.
Today, snow has
taken over.

Yesterday, I sat
on my front porch
basking in
the warm sunshine.

Today, I am relaxing
in my bedroom recliner
with a comforter
covering my legs.

How can the weather
vary so drastically
in such a short
period of time?

I can't change it
so I just accept
whatever weather
comes my way.

After Receiving the Distressing Letter

How can I not be jubilant watching
the robin splashing in the birdbath,
the trillium unfolding beneath the oak?
There will be cruelty. There will be death.
There will be cruelty worse than death.
No need to dwell on that now.
Or later. I have done the best I can do.
Overhead the sky is royal blue and spring's breeze
is fluttering the first leaves dressing the forest.
Tonight, another frost advisory has been posted
and the pansies must be returned to the porch.

The Royal View

To celebrate my ninety-fifth
birthday, Mary and I
climbed the forty-seven steps
to the balcony near the top of
the De Zwaan Windmill
on Windmill Island.

The view was worth
every one of the
forty-seven steps.

First, we looked for
the Jane Tree Corner.
It was a faint spot in
the far distance—
easily recognizable
because of the bridge
beside it.

In another direction
we saw the building where
the park's street organ
music originates
and in another direction
we saw the field
where horses sometimes graze.

I stood there
looking slowly
around me . . .

...

feeling like a Queen
surveying my Queenship.

I was impressed.

Disappointed

It was only a short visit
but I was thrilled
to have Miss Rabbit
here at all.

First thing this morning
Mary and I looked out
my bedroom window
to check if the ducks
were in the pond.
They weren't.

But cuddled up under
the hydrangea bush
under the window
was a rabbit.
She was lying on
her stomach with
her feet stretched
out in front of her.

The rabbit looked
very contented—
like she might
stay there for a long time.

But she didn't.
While I was away
from the window having lunch
she disappeared.
I hoped it was just

...

to find food and
she would return.
She didn't.

Pride

It was her third fall in three years, the young man in the white coat reminded her as he placed a splint on the left wrist. Just days earlier, we'd taped a cheerful video for Marge, the wife of her twin, who'd fallen and broken her hip, whose daughter, after sitting with her mother in the emergency room for eleven hours, was told her mother would not survive surgery and because of COVID would spend her final days alone, who chose, instead, to bring her home in a wheelchair, who arranged for a hospital bed to be delivered to her mother's small condo a few doors from her own, scheduled hospice nurses to provide much-needed pain meds, whose exhaustion I could feel flowing through every cell in my body, the kind of tired that makes you crave a nap in the middle of the day, a nap that extends through nightfall, a nap from which you awaken weary. "Should that happen to you, what decision would you have me make?" I ask Mother at chair chat the following morning. "I want to die before that happens," she responds. And so, we texted the video to the daughter and three days later Mother fell, reinjuring her wrist. The doctor was urging her to transition from a cane to a walker, but pride stood like an enormous snowman blocking the path of reason. On leaving the clinic, we noticed a woman being pushed through the hallway in a wheelchair. Mother decided to name her new maroon-colored walker with oversized, smooth-gliding wheels perfect for outdoor adventures, "Wheelie."

Early Morning

Here comes the Sun
moving slowly
around the corner
of the building
over the pond
through the cattails
into my window
stopping at my feet
as I rest in my recliner.

Thank you, Sun!
You are warm
and welcome
as you soothe
the feet that
walked to the Jane Tree Corner
around Windmill Circle
and climbed The Windmill's
forty-seven steps.

You have given these
ninety-five-year-old feet
the strength and energy
to go on another
grand adventure.

Poets at Play

Seven miles apart
phones in hands
a mother
in the flatlands
edging the city
daughter in the forest
of the dunes
swapping similes
to describe evening skies
like the blush of a magnolia
wings of a fluttering monarch
eggs in the nest of a robin
petals of a long-spur violet
spray of assorted marigolds
face of Annabelle's blossom
gray of the morning fog.
They debate verbs
to describe clouds
hovering
retreating
billowing
swallowing
streaking
whispering
pausing,
as they have done,
to describe
a winter sunset
so different
from their vantage points
yet so much the same.

Total Well-Being

Today I have a feeling
I can only describe
as total well-being.
I am not sure
why I feel as I do.

Could it be because
the world outside my window
is completely white
with new-fallen snow?

Could it be because
this is a free day
with no unwanted tasks
expected of me?

Could it be because
I have no
negative feelings
about anyone anywhere?

Or is it perhaps
all of these things
combined?
Probably so.

When?

I suspect he envisioned
smelling the crisp air of dawn
breaking night's skies over a sleepy lake

as he walked with the retriever
he rescued to be his fishing buddy
to the spot he would make that first cast.

Instead, he fished from a fabric foldup chair,
balance stolen by fate, his dog, Lady,
on a leash held by his wife, daughter nearby.

Perhaps it was better than nothing,
but I doubt that's how he thought his first,
and only, fishing trip with Lady would unfold.

Now, as my seventieth year approaches,
were he alive, he'd ask why I'm waiting.
When I answer, "Mother," I can almost see

his brow crinkle, lips draw tight, hear
his brilliant mind clicking like a calculator,
adding the personal costs incurred

caring for parents, siblings, family,
all the while longing to follow
a whisper of a dream in the fog.

I don't want to walk in his footsteps but
there are times the heavy mist of COVID
swallows everything, including dreams.

...

Until I hear my own whisper; a book
created by mother and daughter
that fills the skies with sunshine

even when it is raining.

A Prized Gift

God said
"Let there be light."
And the glory
of the Sun
was created.

What a wonderful
gift!

On this cold, wintery
Michigan day
I am resting
on my recliner
basking in Sunshine
pouring through
my window.

From the top
of my head
to the tips
of my toes
I am rejoicing
in this marvelous
gift of the Sun.

Thank you, God!

Invisible

We stand together on the sidewalk, eyes closed
to the leafless black branches hiding the sources
of chirps and trills emanating from all directions.

Who says one must see the feathered chests
to experience the euphoria of spring's first sounds?
To feel winter's hardness lift from tired shoulders?

She holds her maroon walker rather than my arm,
safer now on sidewalks cracked and buckled by frost.
While I miss the intimacy of her touch,

it is there, invisible to those driving by,
like the shreds of cattails the red-winged blackbirds
are carefully placing in the midst of the wetlands;

like the distant cooing of the mourning dove
answering the call of one perched overhead;
like the robin's high-pitched whinny that dissolves

into song as we stand, eyes shut, faces raised
to a cloudless sky of royal blue; like the way
we are grateful for the sun's warmth;

like the way I feel her presence
even when she is not at my side.

After the Flight from Albuquerque

A now reoccurring pain
shoots through my pelvic bone
and up my spine when I rise from the chair,
so intense and unfamiliar I catch my breath
and pause before unfolding a body
that has always performed on cue.
Is this what it means to near seventy?

Buds and Birds

There is a softness
and a gentle breeze
on Windmill Island
this special day.

Tiny green sprouts
poke out of the
freshly turned earth
in the flower bed
lining one side
of Jane Tree Corner.

Brownish buds at
the end of each branch
on the Jane Tree
wait patiently to
break through in blossoms.

A red-winged blackbird
perches on a limb
high in the tree
close beside the bench
where we are sitting—
a bench dedicated to
my twin and me.

A short distance away
The Windmill stands
majestically alone
with no visitors in sight.

Only Mary and I
have turned out
to welcome the
First Day of Spring.

Why Am I Here?

Here in this dinky room
stripped to the waist,
given a shirt that opens
in the back, doesn't button,
trapped in a bed with bars,
while people are scurrying
about like squirrels on attack?
You tell me to keep a sense of humor.
Look around.
People masked like bandits
ready to rob me of decency
and who knows what else?
They're poking me for blood,
swabbing inside my nose,
constantly squeezing my arm
with some gizmo that feels
like the first step to amputation.
And don't they talk to each other?
Every person who enters
asks me my name, date of birth,
what year it is, and who's president.
Why don't they look at a calendar?
Turn on TV? And didn't you tell them
we exercise every morning?
No need to repeatedly ask me
to point my finger to theirs,
squeeze their hands, lift my legs.
From the ER to the hospital room,
the same thing over and over.
I'm in great shape,
passed every test perfectly.

Feels like I've been here a month.
Why can't we just go home?
Didn't you tell them
my son drove from North Carolina
to see me? Brought his dog,
Bridget, to meet me?
I'll tell them.
I have to be home by lunch.
Period.

And I was.

That Morning in the Hospital

I might have been a sheet of wallpaper,
flowered and faded, pulled from the walls,
and dropped on a chair at her side. No nod

to my existence. No eye contact. Instead,
the man in the white coat spoke in riddles
to a woman who did not know

and would not remember the medical terms
he tossed so freely in her direction.
My mother does not tolerate rudeness.

Waiting until he paused to breathe, she spoke.
"She is not just my daughter; she is My App."
His head jerked in my direction.

"Do you get it, Mary?"
for often her humor slips by me like
the first hint of a wind shift.

"All Purpose Person. APP.
You are My App."

My Next-to-Best Friend

When I need to
get from one room
to the next
she takes me.

When I need to
put my keys
in a safe place
when I go for a walk
she holds them.

When I want to
sit down briefly
when I'm out on an errand
she holds me.

She's my next-
to-best friend.
She's a walker.
I call her Wheelie.

DAUGHTER

Turning Point

Red, raw and raging. A pain in her throat so severe even a sip of water brings tears to eyes unaccustomed to tears. A cough, dry and rasping at first, travels deep within her lungs, uncontrollable as she tries to breathe night after day after night. Fever. Fatigue. Headache. Words skimmed in newspapers without feeling. Until now. I sit at the foot of Mother's recliner, masked, cheek on folded arms, and pray as I look out her window at the hydrangea we have named "Beauty" and its blossoms: "Peekaboo," "Slash," "Miss In-between," "Miss Hidden," "Miss Proud," "Better-Late." Such fun we have had every morning, greeting the bush and the nearby "Berry-Bird tree," the hanging basket containing "Miss Scarlet," and on the fence, the dangling "Wanderer." There is no fun now. Just fear. Death, I know, is inevitable. But please, not from this virus. I close my eyes. Exhausted. Resigned.

An eerie, unfamiliar silence rouses me.

"I decided to put my mind somewhere else," she whispers. "I have been watching two blossoms on Little Scarlet unfold in the sun. I am better now."

Dear Mother

Someday, when I am unable to sleep
for the emptiness of your recliner,
will you whisper to me in Morse code?

Long and short signals of sound flowing
through the air in rhythmic waves,
letting me know you are okay?

Better still, will you write me a poem
when I face mornings doused in futility
and struggle to get out of bed?

Words and lines and stanzas flowing
through the air in rhythmic waves
so that if I slide down the bed to the floor,

I will again hear your voice? See your smile?
Know that your love stretches far beyond
the window from which you once spoke

of the Berry-Bird tree, the wandering parasol,
conversations with birds, the fluffy blossoms
of hydrangeas, the welcome sight of the sun,

and all that filled your heart with joy each day?
Will you ask my angel to gift me a poem
so I know where and how to find you?

Did you once ask your angel the same?

A Lost Fight

The Sun pours
through the window
covering me with
its warm rays
as I sit
in my recliner
trying to write a poem.

How can I think
when the Sun's warm rays
are insisting
I rest my head
on the back
of my recliner
close my eyes
and clear
my mind completely?

I cannot win a fight
with the Sun's warm rays.

DAUGHTER

A Respite

Alongside ice mountains
created by the fury
of wind and waves
there is a silence
that stills
the heart's agony
so that one might notice
the lone eagle gliding
overhead
and for that moment
be a child again
and fly
alongside.

Lady

Ten years ago today
a special love
went out of
my life—Lady.

She did many
remarkable things
that made her
a special love.

Not only could
she understand
what we said to her
but often she
knew what we wanted
before we spoke.

Perhaps the most
endearing thing
she did for me
was to comfort me
after Dad died.

She could determine
when I was
feeling low and
would rub her chin
up and down my leg.

Of course, she had
a mind of her own,
and sometimes thought
she knew best.

When you walked Lady she was
determined to be the boss.
Whether choosing
where to cross the street
or how fast to walk
Lady made the decision.

It was hard
when Lady died
but she made it
as easy for us
as she could.

One morning
after several days
of feeling sickly,
Lady asked to
go outside.

She went immediately
under her favorite bush
closed her eyes
and never opened them again.

Preparing

Trees turned upside down
by a light so bright I am drawn
to the writing table rarely used,
the one facing west. Normally,
I am a person of the dawn waiting

for melon-streaked skies to reveal
a path through the trees through
which I might jog to the creek
and pause alongside the winterberry
weighted with red fruit and robins.

Mother is writing her obituary,
outlining her memorial,
creating a poem for her death
titled "My Best Friend."
It is a poem about God.

I am writing about the moon.

A Perfect Picture

I see them together—
my husband and Lady—
in a pleasant, peaceful place
somewhere in the Great Unknown.

They take long walks
beside a winding stream,
often stopping to look around
as neither likes to hurry.

Occasionally, Lady dashes
after a rabbit, never really
trying to catch it.
Just to have fun.

Often he brings fishing gear.
Lady watches as he catches
one huge fish after another,
always releasing them back into the water.

Sometimes he takes along
a driver and some golf balls.
He hits long, perfect drives down
the middle of a lush green fairway.

They sit in the shade,
he in a recliner, Lady close by
so he can rest his hand
gently on top of her head.

...

They don't seem to miss me
but I feel they will be happy
to have me join them.
Someday.

Determined

We'd driven long hours to hike Sleeping Bear;
Rubin driving, me, the one longing to hike, alongside.
We arrived to find a parking lot long and empty,
a barricade blocking the entrance, a forbidding

"Closed for the season" sign replacing
the hours of operation. Despite the welcoming
gold of the beeches, red-tipped yellow of the maples,
maroon hue of the oaks, Christmas-green of the pines,

a blanket of white chilled the peak colors of autumn.
I suggested the park's deterrents were for cars, not hikers,
and he, good-natured as always, remained silent
even as northwest winds shook the trees and

wet blobs of snow tumbled from branches overhead.
As we began walking up Pierce Stocking Scenic Drive,
the asphalt covered with snow and falling leaves,
I mentioned how much easier a hike on pavement

than sand and he, my husband of forty years,
mumbled something about all trees
looking the same after an hour, providing
proof to the old adage about opposites.

When we chanced upon the posted trail map
outlining a winding seven-point-three-mile-long road,
a distance I truly did not remember, and he stood quietly
in the sopping cold, we agreed he'd bail halfway.

But I wish he'd been with me when I reached
the Lake Michigan overlook,
not because a large raven, claws spread,
shrill calls emanating from a vicious beak,

kept swooping down inches from my head,
but because Mother Bear, a legend for decades,
revered for keeping vigil for her two lost cubs,
was so much smaller than last I saw her,

barely visible as she perched on a cliff of moraine.
As I whispered goodbye, I wondered if her cubs,
flourishing as islands in a freshwater sea.
had finally let her go.

My Best Friend

When I need someone
to talk to
He listens.

When I share
my closest dreams
He encourages me.

When I admit
my worst faults
He forgives me.

When my heart
is heavy
He lightens it.

When my heart
is light
He blesses it.

He is my
best friend.
He is God.

Epilogue

When I saw the effects COVID's social isolation was having on my mother, the difficult physical and mental changes that occur with age, witnessed the deep sorrow lingering from the deaths of her husband and dog, and years later, from the death of her twin, I introduced the excitement of outdoor adventures into our weekly routine. Walking arm-in-arm through the city and county parks of Holland, Michigan, we laughed, traded memories, discussed birds, flowers, wetlands, rivers, and lakes. But it was one flowering tree, in one park, and one bench, that showed me how nature can heal the spirit, and how important it is to make nature easily accessible to all seniors in all communities.

By 2050, one in four people in the United States will be over the age of sixty. According to a 2007 report issued by the National Institute on Aging and the National Institutes of Health, between 2005 and 2030, the eighty-five-and-over population is projected to increase 151 percent across the globe compared to twenty-one percent for those under sixty-five. While COVID-19 is not reflected in the numbers, chronic diseases such as dementia, Alzheimer's, cancer, cardiovascular disease, arthritis, and diabetes are likely causes of death in those over eighty-five. Such diseases often require long-term care that consumes public and family resources. Worse, the diseases gnaw at the mental and emotional health of seniors and family members.

But nature has the power to heal.

An increasing body of research suggests regular contact with nature can improve short-term memory loss, reduce inflammation, recharge the immune system, diminish a sense of isolation, and lower the overall risk of early death. And it doesn't take that much time. According to one study, just two hours a week can make a difference.

Not all seniors have a retired daughter living seven miles away, able to make nature accessible. Nor does every daughter or son have a parent or grandparent healthy enough to walk the sidewalks and paths of our public parks. And while Mother lives in an apartment with windows opening to wetlands filled with the lively entertainment of red-winged blackbirds and ducks, the soothing sight of water and cattails, not everyone is so fortunate.

Can communities make access to nature easier for the growing senior population?

When we began our outdoor adventures, Mother could walk unassisted for a long mile on any type of path. Over the last eight years, she has transitioned from walking independently to arm-in-arm to cane to walker. Uneven surfaces and cracks matter. So does the slope of the path. Grass, sand or woodchip trails are no longer a possibility; asphalt or concrete is essential. Fear of falling haunts us both.

Over twenty-three public and private parks are within ten miles of Mother's apartment making access to nature possible. But it's not always easy. Favorite spaces boil down to paths, benches, trees, and safety.

Now over ninety-five, Mother needs more frequent pauses and comfortable benches on which to rest, preferably benches shaded by trees that protect eyes sensitive to light and paper-thin skin susceptible to cancer, benches near trees that open the door to sensory stimulation created by leaves that flutter, squirrels that dart, birds that chatter, and a vast array of colors and textures. Research points to the importance of placing benches every ten yards for a senior-friendly park. I've never counted the steps but know that fewer between benches is better with each passing year.

While the majority of parks in our community are clean, wheelchair-accessible with ample parking, there is no "elder space," a designated area where we do not have to worry about children accidentally running into us while chasing a ball, skateboarding or riding a bike. Our favorite park is Windmill Island—not just because of the Jane Tree Corner—but because of the many docents on site who keep "eyes" on visitors to help everyone stay safe. And there are restrooms.

In statistical terms, Mother is an "n" of one. However, I do not think her needs unique. As the senior population mushrooms in our communities, it is to our collective advantage to solicit their input, prioritize their needs and find ways to create a more nature-friendly environment—in the home and out. And while the research shows nature can have a positive effect on one's health, for Mother and me there was more. Nature brought us together on our respective journeys to find inner peace, to live with joy. Such journeys do not stop when one turns sixty-five. If anything, they become more urgent.

We hope *Miracle Within Small Things* will encourage "chats" among seniors and their families, preferably outdoors. To help facilitate such conversations, Mother and I decided proceeds from the sale of our book will go toward providing shaded benches in public spaces in Michigan. We refer to the initiative as "A Bench and a Tree." To learn more, visit https://www.marymckschmidt.com.

Mary McKSchmidt

In Gratitude

There is an intimacy in our relationship that comes, in part, from our shared love of writing, but also from the amount of time we have spent together. Lots and lots of time. That could not have happened without Rubin, a husband willing to share his wife with his in-laws. Just as important, since first meeting them, Rubin has invested in the relationship, creating a friendship that deepened over the decades. His presence enriches all our lives.

It takes a special person to plow through the first draft of a book and provide in-depth feedback. Eric Stemle, Mary's childhood friend, an author and a winner of the Wyoming Teacher of the Year Award for his work with high school students, voluntarily spent massive amounts of time providing written feedback and suggestions. When we were adrift, he offered us direction.

Jack Ridl, the Carnegie Foundation Michigan Professor of the Year and author of several collections of poetry, is a writing mentor and friend. He edited the poems in *Miracle Within Small Things* and enthusiastically supported our efforts. "Landscapes," a group of poets Jack gathers monthly, inspires Mary, provides suggestions, and has been an ongoing source of encouragement.

Thank you to the team at Mission Point Press, particularly Amy Woods Butler, our editor, who believed in us and our ability to weave two different voices into a story that would resonate with adult children and their parents as they navigate the challenges of aging.

To the Comfort Keepers and Atrio caregivers, to the staff at Appledorn West Senior Living Community, Catholic Diocese of Grand Rapids, CPA for Seniors, and to the family members who make it possible for Mother to live independently, with some assistance, we are grateful. A special thanks to daughters/sisters, Kath and Helen, for their thoughts and assistance to Mary and for making it possible for her to take vacations with Rubin.

Most of Mary's friends and cousins have lived through the emotional roller coaster of aging parents and dealt with the sorrow of their passing, as well as the challenges associated with settling their parents' estate. Thank you for listening, caring, and sharing. A special thanks to cousin Jane, daughter of Mother's twin, who continues to walk arm-in-arm with Mary through some of the toughest times, and to her siblings, especially Marcy, who made it possible for Mother to stay in touch with her twin and his wife for as long as they were alive.

Thanks to the editors of the publications where these pieces first appeared: "Beauty in Imperfection" and "Nature's Encore" in *Michigan Blue Magazine*; "A Daughter's Thoughts on Compression Stockings" as the poem of the week in *Hope College Arts Update*; and earlier versions of "The 'Girl' on Windmill Island" and the "Epilogue" in *The Holland Sentinel*.

To the many readers who have read our work, found it beneficial, and encouraged us to keep writing: thank you.

Lastly, to each other . . . know our chair chats are one thread of many that bind us together forever.

Jane McKinney
Mary McKSchmidt

About the Authors

Jane McKinney is the author of nine books, including a children's book, a memoir on motherhood, a collection of essays, and six books of poetry. The mother of six children, she is a former Director of Public Information for the East Lansing School District and a pioneer in the use of cable television in education, for which she won several awards. Her most recent book, *Joy in My Heart*, was published in 2022, the year she turned ninety-six. She is a resident of Michigan and mother of co-author Mary McKSchmidt.

Mary McKSchmidt is an author, photographer, newspaper columnist, and former sports editor. At fifty-three, she gave up her position as a president with Baxter International to pursue her passion: building the political will necessary to clean up and protect the Great Lakes. She appears frequently as a public speaker throughout West Michigan and posts monthly at marymckschmidt. com. Her books include *Uncharted Waters: Romance, Adventure, and Advocacy on the Great Lakes and Tiny Treasures: Discoveries Made Along the Lake Michigan Coast.* She is a resident of Michigan and daughter of co-author Jane McKinney.